The Ideal Candidate
Dominating Life After High-School

PART 1 – All About Me

What's next?

"Success is the progressive realization of a worthy goal or ideal."

Earl Nightingale

The time has come, you've graduated from High-school and it's time to move on to your next endeavor; your new journey. If you are one of the lucky ones, you discovered what you want to do earlier in life. However, if you are like the majority, you know you want to be successful but not quite sure what to do or how to get there. Therefore, it is important for us to sit and understand what success is. By definition, success means the accomplishment of an aim or purpose. My favorite definition of success comes from the Personal Development legend himself, Earl Nightingale; *"Success is the progressive realization of a worthy goal or ideal."*

Let's examine this statement. The first word that stands out in his definition is *"progressive."* By definition, progressive means: happening or developing gradually or in stages; proceeding step by step. This is important and worth focusing on. As humans, we are

always changing, constantly evolving. We also have the control and autonomy to change virtually anything, any time we so desire. For example: how we behave, how we talk, how we dress, the people we hang around, our thought processes, how we handle stress, etc. will all be different, at different stages in our lives. However, one thing is certain at every stage of evolution, at the core, we are always striving to be the best versions of ourselves in life. That's why it's important to focus on progress because you learn that this is a never-ending process. You will forever keep striving to daily to become just a little bit better, with the understanding that you are human, and that perfection is not possible. This helps to put things in perspective. It teaches us to focus on becoming 1% better every day while being patient with ourselves during the inevitable growing pains.

The next word to focus on is "*realization.*" By definition, realization means: (1). An act of becoming fully aware of something as a fact, and (2). The fulfillment or achievement of something desired or anticipated. All of us in life, are just trying to figure it out. Even us, the "*successful adults*" are just as confused about life and what to do sometimes. Life has a funny way of crafting unique obstacles and struggles at

different stages and walk of life. Like a video game, just when you think you've got life figured out, it's moves up a notch higher. This new level will be sure to challenge you in ways you've never been challenged before, forcing out your very best. At each stage in life, it's crucial that we are self-aware. To be self-aware means to have conscious knowledge of one's character, feelings, motives, and desires. Those who are self-aware are typically aware of what they're good at, what they love doing, and what they would want to be doing in both their near and distant futures. The self-aware person is also typically better at making decisions in friendships, relationships, personal finances, and businesses.

To become more self-aware, be sure to follow these steps (pen and paper needed):

1. Find a quiet place.
2. Set a timer for 2 minutes.
3. Write on the paper, "*I am grateful for…*".
4. Start the timer, close your eyes, and meditate on things you are grateful for.
5. Pen down everything that comes to mind.
6. Set timer again for 2 minutes.
7. Now, write on the paper, "*When I picture myself accomplished and happy I see…*"

8. Again start the timer, close your eyes, and meditate on what you see when you are accomplished and happy.
9. Write down everything you pictured, in as much detail as possible. (the more the detail, the better! The more vivid the picture is, the faster you can attract it into your life.)

The next word to focus on is *"worthy."* For something to be worthy, it has to hold some value. In this case, worthy is used as an adjective for *"goal or ideal."* Which means, whatever goals or ideals we've set for ourselves, they should be valuable ones. This is consistent with the thought that innately, we are all striving to be the best version of ourselves. This also helps us in our daily decision making: *is this adding value to my life? Does this action get me closer to my goal? Is this in harmony with my principals and morals?* If the answer is no to any of these questions, chances are, it should be avoided.

Lastly, let's analyze *"goal or ideal."* By definition:

Goal: the object of a person's ambition or effort; an aim or desired result.

Dominating Life After High-School

Ideal: satisfying one's conception of what is perfect; most suitable.

I love this ending because of how well rounded the statement is. As humans, we have a lot we want to accomplish and we all have this image of ourselves at our highest point of happiness that we are constantly striving to attain. When we think about these two words with the adjective "*worthy*" before them, it gets even more interesting. It shows that we need to pursue goals only if they are of value and add value to our lives. And when we look at worthy and ideal, it shows us that we should always be looking to become a person of value. Match that perspective with progressive, and you have a humble approach at constantly looking to add value to yourself and others.

If we are looking at the bigger picture, Earl Nightingale's definition of success tells us just how much in control we really are. We define our own level of success, and no one can do this for us. However, there is a danger with this type of freedom and autonomy: we can set low goals too!

Example:

      Person A: Aims to hit the dartboard 3 times out of 3 attempts. (Succeeded)

      Person B: Aims to hit the Bulls-eye 3 times out of 3 attempts. (Succeeded)

Both person A and person B accomplished their goals. By definition, they are both successful. However, we both know whose accomplishment was more impressive. Person B! It is way more difficult to hit the bulls-eye then to just simply hit anywhere on the board. To avoid making this mistake, we must focus on the goals and ideals that challenge us.

The Challenge of Goal Setting

"Picture yourself in your mind's eye as having already achieved this goal. See yourself doing the things you'll be doing when you've reached your goal." - Earl Nightingale

We must set up goals that challenge us and push us to perform at higher levels. To use an analogy, let's use working out. At the beginner stages of working out, if we don't do enough, we don't get the results.

Conversely, if we do too much too soon, we can injure ourselves and also not get the results we desired. This is where "*progressive*" plays such an important role. To go back to our analogy, often what we can do on day one of a workout transformation is completely different from what we can do on day-90. Therefore, our goals should be different on day one versus day-90. This concept can make it challenging to set goals appropriately. However, the answer hides itself in the problem. Focus on day ninety! When setting goals, focus on the end result! The clearer your vision for day-90 (how you will feel that morning on day-90, what workouts you will do on that day, what your confidence level on day-90 will be, what you will be eating on that day). You will get a clearer roadmap for pulling it off by focusing on the results you wish to attain and experience on day-90.

Measuring Success

"Day-90 is now crystal clear, I'm excited and ready to get started! But wait a minute, what if I go off track? Is there a way I can be more accurate at accomplishing my goals?" The short answer is, YES! We want to set "SMART" goals: *Specific, Measurable, Attainable, Relevant,* and *Time-based*. Any goal that we

set must have these 5 elements. The more detailed we can be when setting the goals, the better.

Example:

Person A: I want to lose weight and feel confident in the gym. (*Abstract. hard to measure*)

Person B: By day-90, I would've lost 8-pounds and tone down to 15% body Fat. (*S.M.A.R.T*)

Both person A and B have the same result in mind, but person B will have an easier time proving to themselves that they accomplished their goals. This helps us to see goal setting in a different way, it's the difference between aiming for the dart board, and aiming for the bulls-eye.

This is where goal-setting starts to shift, and get really interesting. Once the foundation is set, we can easily master the art of SMART goal-setting. This way we can start to effectively set Success Milestones along the way. This allows us to operate at our highest capability and dominate our goal list along the way. It allows us to operate at our highest capability because it provides a framework for us to live by. If we know our goal is to lose 8-pounds by day-90, we know our goal is to be down 3-pounds by day-30 and down 6-pounds

total by day-60. We also know at that rate, we would not only hit our goal, but we could also exceed it by even a pound! This is the value of setting success milestones, it's the roadmap to destination success.

Destination

"People with goals succeed because they know where they're going."

Earl Nightingale

What is my success destination? You may be asking. During my workshops with The Ideal Candidate, this was always the next question. Most of your life up to this point has been structured and guided. No matter what your path in life is after high school, one thing is certain, you will have much more control over your life. Therefore, it is critical that we define your bull's-eye, from the dartboard of life. So, the question is: How do you define success? Take a few moments to ponder on that thought. What does success mean to you?

Let's do a drill designed to help you answer this question:

Steps:

1. Find a quiet room and take a pen and writing pad with you.
2. Set a timer for 5-minutes.
3. Write on the notepad: *"Success for me is:..."*
4. Start the timer, meditate on what Success for you looks like, and visualize happiness.
5. Write down everything that comes to mind.
6. Condense everything you wrote into one sentence that defines your definition of success.

Example: *Success for me is completing the manuscript for my book by the end of 2018 and having 10,000 copies printed and sold by the end of 2019.* (Fingers crossed)

Notice that in this drill, the timeline of the goal or success destination was 1-year. I want to point out that this drill can be used in any timeline that you would like. Personally, I do this drill where I ponder 10-years out, write my answer, 5-years out, write, 1-year out,

write, 6-months out, write, 1-month...and to the present day. I do this quick drill every Sunday to prepare for the weeks ahead. One key note: the timelines should all be congruent with each other. For example, if you see that your goals for 6-months won't get you the results you're looking for in 1-year, it's time to recalibrate and iterate your 6-month plan, 1-month plan, and weekly plan.

Example:

- 1 month: I will finish the manuscript and submit my book for editing
- 6 month: My book will be complete and ready for sale!
- 1 year: I will have sold 10,000 copies!

Notice how the wording is phrased in the sentences above. Your words have to be intentional. You have the power to speak things into existence. In the example above, 1-Year - doesn't say "*I hope to have 10,000 copies sold.*" This type of language doesn't place it in the tangible. The simple difference between saying, "*I hope*" and "*I will*" will make a huge difference when you're doing this drill. It will make an even bigger difference when attracting things into your life.

Reinvent Yourself

"You can't be who you're going to be and who you used to be at the same time!"

Bishop T.D. Jakes

Gratitude

"Be thankful for what you have; you'll end up having more. If you concentrate on what you don't have, you will never, ever have enough."

Oprah Winfrey

Gratitude is the key to true transformation. In fact, having and showing gratitude is so powerful that it positively impacts you and the receiver. Look at this quote from Charles Schwab, *"The way to develop the best that is in a person is by appreciation and encouragement."* Indeed, shifting into what I like to call an *"attitude of gratitude,"* is the fastest way to transform your life. Having an attitude of gratitude helps to shift your perspective. From this new vantage point, it's easier to spot the mini and many blessings in your life. Allow optimism to take over and expect more

and more positive experiences in your life. It's critical that we understand that our thoughts create our reality. That we attract the thoughts and energy we send out into the word. It's in our best self-interest to live a life of gratitude.

Drill: Write down 25 things you are grateful for right now. (It's easier than you think!)

"When I started counting my blessings, my whole life turned around." —Willie Nelson

Purpose

"If you can tune into your purpose and really align with it, setting goals so that your vision is an expression of that purpose, then life flows much more easily." —Jack Canfield

5 Steps to Reinvent Your Life:

1. Create a vision for your future.
2. Write about your reinvention – in details!
3. Surround yourself with visual reminders of the life you'd like to create.
4. Now that you have a vision of your future, break it up into workable tasks.

5. Every day, go back to that vision of you walking toward your future.

Decide. Decide from this moment forward that you will live a life of purpose. I've worked with thousands of students and clients over the years and I've found that a person's purpose can be boiled down to one distinct trait: you are making someone else's life better. So as you go through your journey of life and figure out your purpose, understand that your life will become better, by making someone else's life better. Simple.

(Hint: Life of purpose + attitude of gratitude = recipe for success!)

Life Hack

> **Find Three Hobbies:**

1. **One that makes you money**
2. **One to keep you healthy**
3. **One to keep you creative**

Control Your Thoughts

We must learn to control our thoughts, or we will never be able to learn how to control our behavior. Having control over your thoughts and emotions is a

very valuable and powerful skill to possess. There is a term for purposely modifying your behavior, it's cleverly named *"Behavior Modification."* By definition, it is the direct changing of unwanted behavior by means of biofeedback and/or conditioning.

After high school graduation, you will have a lot more decisions to make daily, and you will typically have less guidance and supervision. This is important to note because we go through much of life through *"Operant Conditioning."*

Operant conditioning is a method of learning that occurs through rewards and punishments for behavior. Through operant conditioning, an individual makes an association between a particular behavior and a consequence. (Skinner, 1938)

To think about it in everyday terms, operant conditioning works like this:

- Bad grades (negative)
  - Punished (decreased behavior)
- Good grades (positive)
  - Rewarded (increased behavior)

Dominating Life After High-School

The problem as we age and develop into successful adults is that this feedback becomes less and less direct. We must learn to discern for ourselves what is positive and beneficial for us and our lives, and what behaviors we would like to embody to attract the "*rewards*" we are looking to experience.

Win Yourself Over Again

1. Appreciate how special you are,
2. Surround yourself with affirmations,
3. Do things you love,
4. Find a replacement,
5. Ditch the self-deprecating humor,
6. Be open to life,
7. Don't compare yourself to others,
8. Forgive yourself,
9. Love yourself.

Remember: Self-control is strength. Mastery can only be attained and experienced through a calm and controlled mind. Eventually, you will gain a level of mastery that guarantees your mood will not shift based on insignificant actions. Never give others the power to control the direction of your life. Never allow your emotions to overpower your intelligence.

"No failure ever cost you as much as your doubt did." -
John Henry

The 4 Agreements from (*The Four Agreements* by Don Miguel Ruiz)

1. Be Impeccable with your word.
2. Don't make assumptions.
3. Don't take anything personally.
4. Always do your best.

"One cannot lead a life that is truly excellent without feeling that one belongs to something greater and more permanent than oneself." — Mihaly Csikszentmihalyi

Science tends to suggest that the secret to becoming a high performer is our deep-rooted desire to direct our lives, enhance our abilities, and make positive contributions to society. From this perspective, we can see that we can build a rich life for ourselves. Where every day that we wake, we do something that matters and that makes someone else's life better. It's not only possible to live your best life and live a life of service; it's the goal.

A Theory of Human Motivation

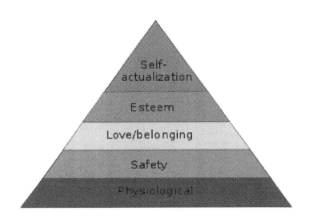

8 Things to give up

1. Doubting Yourself,
2. Negative Thinking,
3. Fear of Failure,
4. Criticizing Yourself and Others,
5. Negative Self Talk,
6. Procrastination,
7. Fear of Success,
8. People Pleasing.

"When you brand yourself appropriately, the competition becomes irrelevant." – John Maxwell

PART 2

<u>TOOLBOX</u>

Welcome to the Success Toolbox.

This toolbox is designed to be your guide and reference on your road to success. Please come to this section any time you would like to learn and refresh your skills.

Your Toolbox includes:

- Financial Literacy,
- Table Manners,
- Corporate Integration,
- Effective Communication,
- Dress For Success,
- Health,
- Real Estate.

You don't have to read this section in any particular order. Pick the option that interests you and gets started. This section is structured to give you the

autonomy to learn in your own way, and robust enough to return to again and again for continued learning.

Financial Literacy

If you are like me, you have ambitious goals for yourself and your life after high school. I must say, I am proud of all that I was able to accomplish from high school graduation to age 24. I played soccer for Lincoln College from 2007-2009 (the worst economic downturn in decades). During this economic downturn, my parents couldn't afford to send me sufficient money for groceries, toiletries, college fun (let's be honest!). So to make up for this, I decided to start cutting hair for some side income. After graduating with my Associates Degree, I continued my education at Lewis University while I completed my Bachelor's degree and another year of soccer (our team ranked 3rd in the nation NCAA Division II, I've got the trophy to prove it!).

Senior year rolled around and I wasn't getting as much playing time as I wanted, and my coach didn't think I'd earned a scholarship, so I decided to quit soccer and focus on my entrepreneurial dreams. In my senior year, I started my first company, an event

company called Red Tie Events while working full time as a waiter/bartender for TGIFridays.

Fast forward to graduating from Lewis University, I stopped bartending and got my first *"adult"* position as an administrative assistant and still running my event company; it was churning out profit from 2 events a week and promotions. Relative to age 22, I was doing quite all right....this as it turns out...was a recipe for disaster. I was riding on a high, with no financial structure or guidance and the wave was sure to take me under if I didn't do something fast. This was the most money I had ever made in my life, and I had 2 streams of income! Why not do what I want? And that is exactly what I did. I was living the high life: lavish dates, hotel rooms (I was still living with my parents! Ha!), a brand new car, concerts, sporting events, all the new clothes and suits. This lifestyle did take its toll on my account, and I noticed my credit card debt had started to rise...and that's when I got the call. I got the job! Overnight, I would be making about $17,000 more than I was already making; my debt problems were solved. Wrong! The problem was I didn't have the right habits and disciplines in place, I pacified the problem for a second, but the new income only made me more comfortable.

Then, the impossible happened. One rainy Monday morning, I walked into the office and saw multiple people crying and my stomach dropped. "Kevin, can you meet me in my office," my boss said....I was one of 25 others to be laid off due to budget constraints. I was sick to my stomach. Fast forward 3 months from getting fired: I was 24 years old, I had done "everything right," at least that's what I thought. Yet I was unemployed, $18,000 in debt (not counting student loans!), and with a car in repossession.

THIS is why I developed the Financial Literacy course, so my students don't make the same mistakes I once did. Since that date, I've taken the time to study money. How it works, how it's earned, how to invest it, how to keep it. I've studied multiple books, attended numerous seminars, been fortunate to be mentored by financial specialists, and worked in the socio-economic development field with Chicago Neighborhood Initiatives and Chicago Urban League. Even now, there is much more to learn and the landscape is always changing. So understand that as you start this journey, there truly isn't a destination. This module is designed to provide a framework for your financial literacy decisions in the real world. This is essentially, everything

I wish someone taught me before I graduated high school.

Cash Flow

Cash Flow: This is the relationship between monthly income and expenses.

To create a positive cash flow, you need to spend less then you earn. Simple (not really!). To accomplish this, we need to master the art of budgeting and create a spending plan.

What a spending plan will do for you:

- Allows you to learn how finances work in life.
- Enables you to make good decisions about how you use money.
- Makes you aware of where your money is going.
- Gives you a way to save for specific items.
- Helps you to live within your income – or decide if you need to increase it.
- Shows you where to cut spending.
- Provides methods for keeping good records of spending.

- Allows you to spend money without feeling guilty.
- Creates a way to measure your progress.

Assess Needs – Needs vs. Wants

We must make a realistic list of needs and wants. Needs are things like: Food, Clothing, Housing, Transportation, Child Care, Insurance, Medicines, etc. Needs are exactly how they sound, it's an absolute necessity. This would typically fulfill the lowest tier in Maslow's Hierarchy. Wants on the other hard are things such as Event tickets, Big TV, New Car, Designer Jeans, Vacations, Jordans. Do I have to explain it further? You get the point. And in order to accomplish your goals, it's critical to have this skill to decipher between needs and wants and the discipline to sacrifice your wants in pursuit of your financial goals.

Set Goals and Make a Plan

Make sure your goals are smart:

- Specific – Clearly state what you want to do

- Measurable – Measure by time and/or money needed
- Attainable – Make Sure your goal is realistic and possible
- Relevant – Make sure goals fit your needs
- Time-related – Set a definite target day (day/month/year)

Put things in order of priority. Imagine the actions you need to take to get from where you are now, to where you want to be. Goals are dreams with deadlines! Post your goals where you will see them frequently. Find a picture to represent your goals. Make a vision board for yourself. Seeing your goals consistently has a positive effect on the mind. Make your goals happen!

Smart Goal Example:

Goal: Purchase a refrigerator in 6-months - $600.

Must Save From Each Paycheck

- $100/paycheck – if paid monthly
- $50/paycheck – if paid bi-weekly or semi-monthly

- $25/paycheck – if paid weekly

To keep this simple, money management can typically be broken down into two distinct sides: INCOME and SPENDING. The money that comes in, your regular take home pay, is your income. The money that goes out, your expenses, is spending. You must know what you are spending to develop a plan for managing our money.

Income

Income has two parts: Gross and Net. Gross income is the total you actually earn. Net income (take home pay) is what is left over after your employer takes out deductions for taxes, Social Security, Medicare, and other needs/fees. This should help spread more light on Drake's line when he said, "*Open the mail, staring at the check. It's enough to make you throw up, it's gross what I net.*" Drake is proving his financial savvy in this clever line. Next, we move forward to the spending section.

Expenses

There are typically three types of expenses: Fixed Expenses, Flexible (or variable), and Seasonal (or occasional) expenses.

A fixed expense is an expense that will be the same total amount regardless of changes in the amount of sales, production, or some other activity. Examples of fixed expenses are: Car Payments, Rent or Mortgage, Childcare, Cable TV, Car Insurance.

Flexible expenses are costs that are easily changed, reduced or eliminated. Spending money on entertainment and clothing represent flexible expenses. Even expenses that must be incurred, such as a grocery bill, can be considered flexible because the amount spent can vary. More examples of flexible expenses are: clothing, utilities, gasoline, public transportation, medical/dental, and supplies.

Seasonal or occasional expenses are expenses that you know you will have at some point throughout the year, but they won't directly affect your month to month spending plan. For example, if you own a vehicle, you know that you must renew the city stickers annually. It would also be wise to start saving for car maintenance and repair issues. One tricky one we always like to point out here is holidays! My mother would never stress about Christmas presents like some of the other parents I would talk too. Years later after asking why, my mother said she would start saving for Christmas in January! So by the time, it was December 1st, she was

typically done shopping already and did it without any stress. This is the power of having a spending plan. You can design the life you want, stress-free. (Vacations are also considered an occasional expense, travel with ease my friends!)

Tracking your money

Keep and organize the following items to help you keep up with your expenses:

- Check Stubs
- Canceled checks
- Receipts
- Bills
- Invoices
- Credit Card Statements
- Calendars
- and Pocket Notebooks

Trimming Expenses

One of the biggest challenges in personal finance is figuring out ways to spend less money. One of the best ways to accomplish this is to cut down on your monthly expenses. Even though some of our regular bills might seem small and insignificant on their own, their cumulative effect can be enormous. If we are not

careful and conscious of our spending habits, this can become a huge drain on our resources. Our goal then should be to minimize the damage caused on a monthly basis. We must look for ways to cut expenses that are effective and easy to implement.

Below, you will find a few ways to save money, that shouldn't be too cumbersome to accomplish, but offer the potential to save huge sums of cash over time:

- Pack Lunch for work or school
- Shop the store or generic brands
- Use the public library
- Choose free recreational activities
- Eat out less often
- Handle home maintenance and repairs yourself
- Use public transportation when possible
- Take advantage of free activities

"Beware of little expenses. A small leak will sink a great ship." – Benjamin Franklin

Credit

The definition of credit is: The ability of a customer to obtain goods and services before payment, based on the trust that a payment will be made in the future.

Credit is when goods, services, or money is received in exchange for a promise to pay a definite sum of money at a future date.

Why is good credit important?

Your credit history shows how you've managed your finances and repaid your debts over time. Your personal credit report is a listing of the information in your credit history. This begins the first time you apply for credit. From that point on, each time you apply for a credit card or loan, and the subsequent payments. All of these information are included in your credit report. **The most important component of your credit report is whether you make payments on time.** Anytime that your credit report shows a Late Payment – *30 days, 60 days, or 90 days* – a **"red flag"** is raised and you may be denied credit or pay more interest if you get it.

A good credit history increases the confidence of those in a position to loan you money, like creditors (also known as lenders). When they see that you have paid back your loan when and how you agreed, they are more likely to extend credit again. With good credit, you can borrow for major expenses, such as a car, home, or education. Also, you can borrow money at a lower cost with a good credit score.

High Score, Low Cost vs. Low Score, High Cost

The better your credit, the lower the cost of credit. A good credit score makes you more eligible for lower interest rates and fees. This means you will have more money available for saving and spending and lenders will have more confidence in your ability and commitment to repay the loan on time and in full.

Bad Credit History

If your credit is not good, you will probably pay higher interest rates and fees which means you will have less money available for savings and spending. Over time, higher rates and fees translate into the loss of literally thousands of dollars of potential savings.

Example of how good credit report saves money:

$10,000 Auto Loan, 5 Year Term

Credit Score	Interest Rate	Monthly Car Payment	Total Interest Paid
Low	25%	$294	$7,611
Okay	12%	$222	$3,347
Excellent	5%	$189	$1,323

In the example above, you can see the benefits of having a good credit score. All 3 of these people bought the same car, for the same price, for the same term. However, the person with a low credit score paid $4,264 more than the person with an average score and $6,288 more in interest then the person with an excellent score...*FOR THE EXACT SAME CAR*!

Inquiries and Your Credit Score

When you apply for credit, you authorize the lender to ask for a copy of your credit report – an inquiry or "Hard Pull." When someone does a "Soft Pull," this means that they check your credit score without impacting your credit score. A "Hard Pull" on the other hand, will impact your credit score and the "inquiry" will be visible on your credit report. Your credit score may drop a few points when you apply for new credit. Most credit scores are not affected by multiple inquiries from auto or mortgage lenders within a short period of time - usually 30 days. In these cases, multiple inquiries will be treated as a single inquiry, and this will have little or no impact on your credit score.

Revolving vs. Installment Debt

Definition:

- Installment Debt: a set loan amount paid over time with a fixed payment schedule. (Example: House Mortgage)
- Revolving Debt: a debt instrument that can be charged up to a limit, paid down, and then charged back up again. (Example: Credit Cards)

Installment debt allows a borrower to finance a large, secured purchase whereas installment debt allows borrowers flexible options for making smaller, unsecured purchases. This means that installment debts are typically easier to budget for, while revolving debt payments can be trickier because the payments tend to vary from month to month, based on charges.

Credit Scores

What is a credit score or FICO Score? Simply put, it's a prediction of how likely you are to pay your bills. Your credit score number will be between 300 and

850 derived from many different factors. This is the number that drives the approval of credit extensions and the interest rate you pay on those extensions.

The FICO scoring model looks at more than 20 factors in five categories:

- How you pay your bills (35%)
- Amount of money you owe and the amount of available credit (30%)
- Length of credit history (15%)
- Mix of credit (10%)
- New credit applications (10%)

Range of Scores

The following are some basic guidelines for interpreting a credit score:

- 300-620 – Poor Credit
- 621-690 – Fair Credit
- 691-720 – Good Credit
- 721-750 – Good to Excellent Credit
- 751-800 – Excellent Credit
- 801-850 – Nearly Perfect Credit

What Doesn't Impact My Credit?

Not everything gets reported on your credit. One question we get asked consistently is debit card purchases. Debit cards act as plastic checks; the money is removed from the checking account immediately and does not report to the credit bureau. Prepaid cards typically will not report to credit bureaus; however "Primor Cards" are prepaid cards that WILL impact your credit score. The prior card is essentially a prepaid debit card that reports to the credit bureau like a credit card. This is the safest way to effectively build credit with little risk. Another tricky area is utility and phone bills. Utility and phone accounts in good standing (meaning you are paying on time and as agreed) will not report to the credit bureau.

However, if the account goes into collections (meaning you are 90 days "red flags" past due) then they will send this debt to collections and this will be reported on your credit report and your score will be negatively impacted as a result. Another subtle difference is renting vs. owning. Rent payments aren't automatically tracked on your credit report, but mortgage payments are. The reason is because you had to take a loan out on the mortgage, and you didn't pay for the rent payments. However, you can take the time to manually report your rent payments and these

payments will positively impact your scores. The difference is, you must take the initiative to do so, and you cannot report this yourself. You must ask your landlord to do this as proof for you. It can be a hassle, but it's 100% worth your time to do so.

Second Resume

Think of your credit report as a second resume. A credit report contains information about where you work, live, how you pay your bills, whether or not you have filed bankruptcy and if you have ever been arrested or sued. You can check your credit score for free up to three times annually at: **http://www.annualcreditreport.com**

Use Credit Wisely

For decades, society has promoted the idea of "buy now, pay later." This is a good concept for some types of purchases and a bad concept for many other types of purchases.

Credit Card Advantages:

- Convenient
- Useful for emergencies

Dominating Life After High-School

- Often required to hold a reservation
- Ability to purchase expensive items sooner
- Eliminates the need to carry large amounts of cash
- Taking advantage of the perks and incentives

Credit Card Disadvantages:

- Paying Interest
- Additional fees are common
- Temptation to overspend
- Can cause large amounts of debt
- Identity theft

Good credit purchases are things like purchasing a house or financing your education. Buying a house on credit is a smart move as home values rise quickly and you can gain equity through appreciation. Financing your education is also a good investment in the future. Your earning potential will eventually outweigh the cost of tuition, and educational loans are usually at a very low-interest rate. Even buying a car can be a good credit purchase if you need it to get back and forth to work, etc. It is important to make sure not to

get caught up in buying a vehicle for more than you can afford. Stick to your spending plan!

Bad credit purchases, such as credit card debt and other consumer debt are the worst type of debt. Interest rates and fees on borrowing money this way will be the highest of all, mostly because there is rarely a tangible item as collateral. Similar to the example in good credit purchase, financing a car for longer than the life of the vehicle can also be an unwise credit decision.

Laying the Right Financial Foundation

Credit cards are a great concept, but they end up bringing financial ruin to many people who do not use them properly (remember my college story!). Never use credit cards as extra money. Always allocate money from your current funds or monthly income in order to immediately pay off whatever you finance. Tip: read the fine print! Make sure to take the time to read the fine print on the agreement, and make sure you are getting the best terms available.

American consumers ages 20-29 carry an average of $5,781 in revolving debt. This would take 11 years and 4 months to pay off assuming an average interest rate of 13% and the minimum payments are made.

A credit card is a responsibility. The choices you make now will affect how much you pay for your car, your home, and any other loans or credit cards you apply for.

Saving

It is never impossible to save money, no matter how small the amount. When opening a savings account, there are typically 2 accounts you will open: Emergency Fund and Nest Egg Account. The emergency fund provides a means for paying for emergencies instead of using credit. On the contrary, a nest egg account helps you reach specific goals, such as buying a house or taking a vacation. This is where things get fun and you start to see the true benefits of planning ahead and being disciplined in your execution. Just think, if you save $20 per week, every week for a year after one year you will have saved $1,040! Keep this up and after five years you will save $5,200. Not to mention, this is where the wealthy start to really "play the system."

Many people will open up an interest-earning savings account. So imagine if we saved the $5,200 in

your savings account at 2.20% interest, you would've earned $114.40 of "free" money. This number might seem small, but let's look at another example for comparison. If we would've invested $52,000 at 2.20% that would be $1,144 of "free money." This is how "the rich get richer" and "let their money work for them." Having an interest-earning savings account is a smart

way to accelerate your financial goals.

As we mentioned above, one of the easiest ways to save is by trimming your expenses and saving the excess income from your efforts. Below is a breakdown of ways to save and the positive compound effect of applying this strategy.

Example 1: (work average 22 days/month)

Lunch	$10	$220/Month
Coffee	$3	$66/Month
Soft Drinks	$2	$44/Month
Child's Lunch	$4	$88/Month

Total: $418/Month and **$5,016/Annually**

Dominating Life After High-School

Example 2: (work average 22 days/month)

Lunch	$5	$110/Month
Coffee	$1.50	$33/Month
Soft Drinks	$1	$22/Month
Child's Lunch	$2	$44/Month

Total: $209/Month and **$2,508/Annually**

Remember These Tips:

- Don't shop on payday.
- Don't shop when you're tired.
- Don't shop for food when you're hungry.
- Take your time! Try not to shop when you have to hurry.
- You don't have to buy today.
- Remember, nothing is necessary unless you need it.
- No one can make you buy anything.
- Have a spending plan and stick to it!

Balance spending and saving, set goals and develop a plan. - Get the most from your money!

"Financial literacy is just as important in life as the other basics." John W. Rogers Jr.

Table Manners

"Good manners will open up doors that the best education cannot." – Clarence Thomas

This section is a guide to eating in a timeless style.

Proper Posture

Posture is very important, especially at the dinner table. We must make sure we are sitting up straight at the table and conscious of not hunching over our food. Having a good posture will communicate confidence and competence at the dinner table, but it also has a host of other benefits. Sitting up straight helps to relieve back and neck tension, it increases our oxygen intake and even helps to prevent overeating. On the flip side, a bad posture has the reverse effect. Hunching over your food strains your neck, shoulders, back, and abs. It also restricts your breathing and encourages overeating! Make sure that we have a

proper posture throughout dinner and make sure that you are taking food to your mouth, instead of bringing our mouth to the food.

In the Driver's Seat

We understand that formal banquet dinners can be a bit intimidating. We sit down in front of 3 different size plates, a soup bowl, 2 forks, 2 spoons, and different cups/glasses. It can be confusing to know which plate or glass is yours at this round table. Well, we have a trick for that to help you remember! Every time you're at formal dinner, I want you to picture yourself in the driver's seat of a BMW. This is an acronym to help you remember. B stands for Bread, M stands for Meal, and W stands for Water.

There are a set of rules and this is the first trip. Whenever you sit down, your bread plate will always be the smallest plate and it will always be placed on your left-hand side, usually above the meal plate (Please note: the bread plate can also be placed on top of your meal plate). Your meal plate will always be placed directly in front of you. And your water is always to the right, always. If you ever get lost on whose water is whose, picture yourself in the driver's seat.

Bread Etiquette

Dominating Life After High-School

I know what you're thinking, *"Kevin, really? There are rules to eating bread?"* Yes! Absolutely there are! So, let's dive into the exciting world of buttering and eating your dinner roll. If the bread is placed in front of you, feel free to pick up the basket and offer it to the person on your right. If the load is not cut, cut a few pieces, offer them to the person to your left, and then pass the basket to your right. Do not touch the load with your fingers; instead, use the cloth in the bread basket as a buffer to steady the bread as you slice it.

Place the bread and butter on your butter plate, yours is on your left, then break off a bite-sized piece of bread, put a little butter on it, and eat it. **Don't butter the whole piece of bread and take bites from it!** Don't hold your bread in one hand and drink in the other. Another polite rule to follow, don't take the last piece of bread without first offering it to others.

Is that oil?!? In some restaurants, olive oil is served with the bread. In these cases, pour a small dose of oil onto your bread plate (it's common to add salt, pepper, and even cheese to the oil). Once the oil is ready, dip your bite-sized pieces of bread in the oil and enjoy!

Handling Utensils

The continental table manners style prevails at all meals, formal and informal because it's a natural, non-disruptive way to eat.

1. Hold your fork in your left hand, tines downward.
2. Hold your knife in your right hand, an inch or two above the plate.
3. Extend your index finger along the top of the blade.
4. Use your fork to spear and lift food to your mouth.
5. If your knife is not needed, it remains on the table.

Passing The Food

Pass to the right. Simple. One diner either holds the dish as the next diner takes some food, or he hands it to the person, who then serves him/herself. Heavy dishes are put on the table with each pass. Special rules apply to passing salt and pepper and passing bread and butter. The general rule here with bread and salt/pepper, always pass to the right the first time, after that, you can pass in the fastest direction of the individual who asked.

Appropriate Dinner Conversation

"Worse than talking with a mouthful is gossiping with a mouthful!" — Anthony Liccione

The first tip we can provide here is to listen more than you speak. Ironically enough, the key to the art of conversation is not in the talking, but in the listening. Avoid the common mistake of talking about yourself too much. This is very easy to do and makes us seem self-centered. The easiest way to avoid this mistake is by asking engaging questions to let the person know we are interested in the conversation. Ask those you converse with interesting and thoughtful questions. People love to talk about themselves, let them. Don't just ask what someone does and leave it at that. Take things a step further. Ask them what the hardest part of their job is or how the future of their profession looks. Then go even further and ask follow-up questions from the information they disclose. This is the best way to fish out more details and quickly make friends at the dinner table. Let your guests know you are genuinely interested in focusing on who's talking, nodding your head, and adding "hmmms,"

"interesting!", and "uh-huhs" at the appropriate moments.

Pause! Before you open your mouth to speak, stop and think about what you are going to say. Too many people speak before they think, and when the words come out, they don't convey the intended meaning. Pause a moment to allow your internal filters to take over. This may be the difference between appearing as a good conversationalist and making a boorish or uneducated impression.

Ideas for discussion topics:

- Local News Items
- Sports
- Favorite Books
- Hobbies
- Pop Culture Topics
- TV Shows or movies
- New Businesses in the area.

Put the phone away

Texting and/or constantly checking your phone for messages, social media updates, etc. will send the wrong message. No one wants to feel that the phone is

more important than the here and now conversation. Put your phone on silent, put the phone away, and stay present in the moment.

Be Aware of Body Language

We must be aware of our body language and the body language of others. Non-verbal clues will leave signs that the receiver will pick up on. Here are some signs that the other person is no longer engaged in the conversation (or you are not engaging):

- Yawning
- Stops making eye contact
- Glancing around the room looking for an escape
- Starts backing away
- Stops responding

Take Your Time

Let's remember to take your time through the meal and enjoy the entire process. Don't rush through your meal, or get lost in the conversation of it all. Remember to chew with your mouth closed and speak after swallowing all of your food. Be conscious of your body language when speaking and be mindful that you aren't waving your utensils while speaking. If you would

like more of something, don't reach over someone else's food, politely asked the person next to you and wait patiently for the dish to be passed to you. Take your time through the process, and be observant of those around you. If you are ever lost about what to do in a situation, be patient, and wait to see what others at the table are doing.

Top 10 Table Manner Tips:

- Place your napkin in your lap
- Turn off your phone
- Wait for everyone to be served before eating
- Use a knife and fork to cut meat
- Cut your food one piece at a time
- Chew with your mouth closed
- Don't reach across the table
- Don't talk with your mouth full
- Don't pick your teeth at the table
- Say "excuse me" when leaving the table

Part 3 - Designing My Life

Health

"To keep the body in good health is a duty, otherwise we shall not be able to keep our mind strong and clear." Buddha

When it comes to health, it helps me personally when I think of myself as a spirit that is inhabiting a physical body. From this perspective, I can see that I need my body to interact with and experience the world. If I take that thought a step further, I can see that my body has to be in the best condition possible at all times. So that I can live my best life, at all times. Think about the times when you've fallen ill. Chances are, nothing else mattered at that time. You couldn't enjoy your family, your friends, your money, your food, or your life the same way. Below is a quick 3 point checklist and guide to staying healthy.

Check Point 1 - Mind:

Everything starts in the mind. If you are going to have a healthy mind and body, you have to believe you have a strong and healthy mind and body. We've seen the placebo effect work. We've seen cancer and other

THE IDEAL CANDIDATE
Dominating Life After High-School

physical ailments reversed/cured miraculously. Never underestimate the power of a strong and controlled mind.

I started my journey to mental domination after I was sick and tired of feeling lost — my personal story. I was born with ADD and Dyslexia, so reading and focusing for me was very difficult growing up. I struggled with this my entire life. It wasn't until I said "enough is enough" and decided to do something about, that my life changed. I started first with meditation and breathing exercises for about 15 minutes a day so that I could calm and still my mind. Next, I started reading 15 minutes a day, rain or shine, busy or bored. Within 1 year, I was able to meditate on demand for long periods of time and I was reading about 5 books a year. Fast forward to date at 29 years old as I write this book, I read 18 books last year while juggling my full-time job, part-time job, my company Success Hub, and my nonprofit The Ideal Candidate.

Never underestimate your capabilities and the power of a strong, healthy still mind.

Check Point 2 - Body:

Eating poorly is like buying everything on credit: one day you will pay for it. It's critical that we are conscious of our health decisions. Our foods should be replenished on a cellular level. We should consume alkaline water and getting plenty of sleep at night.

(Side Note: I am NOT a fan of "Team No Sleep." Although they were absolute nights when I purposely stayed up late and woke up early to get a big project done. This is acceptable. But consistent behavior of only getting minimal sleep is a recipe for disaster. Our minds and our bodies need adequate sleep in order to function at their highest level.)

Quick Tips for a healthy body:

- Drink plenty of water (Alkaline if you can!)
- Eat for health (I hate vegetables, so I make them into a smoothie/juice every day)
- Exercise 3-5 hours a week (Or more for the ambitious!)

- ☐ Get a massage (This helps to release toxins and stress from our body)
- ☐ Meditate (Try it! It's fantastic for your body and mind)
- ☐ Stretch! (Helps release stress from our body, no more Charley Horses!)

Check Point 3 - Spirit:

Once again, this reflects my perspective of us being spiritual beings inhabiting a physical body. It's critical that we are feeding and loving our spiritual needs as well. Travel to a new location, try new food, try new experiences, make new friends, and read a new book. Our spirit comes alive right outside our comfort zones. It's important for us to push the limits the comfort and keep expanding so that we are living our best life.

Dating

"Find someone you can build with while providing each other peace." - Kevin P. Davenport

News Flash: The person you date, is a direct reflection of you. I wish someone had told me this sooner as I didn't realize this until much later in life. Don't believe me on this topic? Maybe you'll listen to

the 3rd wealthiest man in the world, Multi-Billionaire Warren Buffett, *"The most important decision you'll ever make has nothing to do with money or career, the biggest decision of your life is who you choose to marry."* After research, psychologists from Carnegie Mellon University agreed with Warren's perspective saying that who you marry can significantly affect your level of success. The bottom line is, people with supportive partners are much more likely to give themselves a chance to succeed. Even as we consider the quote, *"You are the sum of the 5 people you spend the most time with."* Your significant other will probably be the number 1 person you spend time the most.

We don't want to spend too much time on this topic, but we encourage everyone to think long and hard about their dating decisions and understand that this area is much more impactful in your life then you may have originally considered. The very first step in making a good choice in this department is understanding YOUR worth first. Once you understand your worth and the goals you want to accomplish in life, choosing the right partner becomes a little bit easier. Choose wisely, have fun, and be respectful in your dating life.

Dating Etiquette 101 - Quick Tips:

Dominating Life After High-School

1. Men should open doors for women.
    a. At a revolving door, the gentleman should go slightly ahead and push the revolving door for the woman and then let her walk in first.
2. Men should walk on the inside of the street.
3. Men should let women off the elevator first.
4. Men and Women should give each other complete and undivided attention. (Put the phones away.)
5. Be on Time. (This is a good rule in all walks of life.)
6. Make Eye Contact.
7. Be mindful of dominating the conversation, be respectful of each person's opinions.
8. Ask Questions. (Especially follow up questions to dig deeper into the current subject.)
9. Dress to Impress.
10. Don't dwell on your ex.

Living On My Own

"Ninety percent of all millionaires become so through owning real estate." – Andrew Carnegie

Dominating Life After High-School

For many of you, this is or will be soon your first time living on your own. I remember my thoughts when I first moved into my dorm room and I remember when I finally moved into my first apartment. At that time, all I could see was all the fun I'd have. You know the typical story: staying up late, having friends over, doing basically what I want. This is all true, but I want to shine a light on the entire picture. I want to go back and give you the advice I would've wanted to hear, straight and to the point. Here we go.

Magical Toothpaste

I remember going up, the toothpaste would just appear one day. One day it was getting low...and boom, new toothpaste there. It wasn't until I got into college that I realized just how much little things added up:

Here's a quick list of one time purchases that you probably aren't prepared for living on your own: plates, bowls, cups, utensils, rug, microwave, hangers, iron, ironing board, hamper, wastebasket.

Here's a quick list of recurring purchases that you probably aren't prepared to handle while living on your own: soap, shampoo, conditioner, garbage bags, toothpaste, contact solution, batteries, paper towels, toilet paper, laundry detergent.

Get mentally prepared to plan and budget for these new obligations.

Rent Vs. Home Owner

"Owning a home is a keystone of wealth... both financial affluence and emotional security."

– Suze Orman

There are many different thoughts on when is the best time to purchase a home. I can't say that there is a right way or time to do anything, but I do want to encourage more home ownership in black and brown communities. I also believe that homeownership is one of the best ways to build wealth. It is precisely why I am in the process of purchasing my first property at 29 years old. Quite honestly, I feel like I am way behind the ball. I am meeting more and more of my peers that are my age or younger and own multiple properties. If I could go back and do it all over again, I would've stopped renting a long time ago, and considered purchasing a property sooner. If I had one tip to give you in this department: live below your means in your 20's. There are many Americans that are *"house poor,"* living in a place too expensive for them to live

comfortably. My favorite book on the topic is: *Millionaire Real Estate Investor* by Gary Keller.

Leadership

"The first person you lead is you." – John C. Maxwell

The Four Phases of Leadership Growth by John C. Maxwell:

1. I Don't Know What I Don't Know

2. I Know What I Don't Know

3. I Grow And Know It

4. I Simply Grow Because Of What I Know

I love John's simple breakdown of this because it shows the relationship between value, knowledge, and leadership. These three traits are truly connected. We see the patterns over and over. No matter what we do in life, there is always a learning curve, the time it takes to go from beginner to mastery.

For a newborn, this is what John Maxwell's list would look like:

1. Crawl

THE IDEAL CANDIDATE
Dominating Life After High-School

2. Stand
3. Walk
4. Run

This can be applied to any new endeavor and Leadership is no different. Leadership is the ability to motivate and influence others to the desired outcome. Leaders have a vision and a deep belief in themselves that allows for sound decision making and the ability to set direction. The beauty of leadership and most of the skills that we discussed in this book is that they can be learned and developed! We can learn from watching others (good and bad examples! Sometimes a bad example makes a bigger impact than a good one.), taking classes, experience, or purposeful reading like you're doing now.

Now that we've laid the foundation of the leadership learning process. Let's dive into the "ingredients" of a good leader. To be a good leader, you will need 5 distinct ingredients: Communication, Awareness, Integrity, Relationship Building, and Leadership Building.

Communication: This is the starting point for connection. We can't lead without being seen, heard, or felt.

THE IDEAL CANDIDATE
Dominating Life After High-School

Awareness: Leaders constantly observe, reflect, and learn. This practice allows them to predict patterns and helps to accelerate the leadership growth process.

Integrity: All leaders have a foundation of respect and trust. This comes from being honest, taking responsibility, and doing the right thing consistently.

Relationship Building: "Life is not about what you know, but who you know."

Leadership Building: Building other leaders is a true sign of leadership. In return, over time, the leader is surrounded and supported by other leaders who are immensely valuable to him/her, because he/she invested in them.

"The people we encounter may not have interacted with anyone else living as purposely and authentically as we are, so every opportunity is a chance for us to demonstrate, respond with and teach love, compassion, purpose, and authenticity!"

Renita D. Alexander

(Visualization Files)

Kevin's Top 10 Tips for Success

1. Consistency

Almost everything that has value in life is a product of consistency. If only people understood how powerful and important it is to be consistent. Success, Health, Fitness, Wealth, Relationships, and all other aspirations and goals are all about consistency.

"We are what we repeatedly do. Excellence, then, is not an act, but a habit." - Aristotle

2. Reflect

Get into the habit of asking yourself, "Does this support the life I'm designing?" This should be asked in every realm of your life: family, relationships, jobs, opportunities, events, etc. Take at least 15 minutes a day to find a quiet place with no distractions, and reflect on your day. Ask probing questions like how and where can I improve? How you would handle a similar situation next time it comes around. Reflect on what you really want for your life. Reflect on what truly makes you happy and filled with purpose and warmth.

Tip: If it's not in alignment with your long term goals and vision, then it is dead weight!

3. Show Gratitude

The best way to gain more support in life is to show gratitude. Gratitude opens doors to more relationships. It's also been shown to improve your physical and psychological health. Having and showing gratitude helps to improve your self-esteem and open your heart to be more empathy reducing aggression. In short, gratitude helps us to celebrate the present.

4. Choose Wisely

In essence, you make your choices, and your choices make you. Everything from your daily habits, diet, friends, and even the entertainment you choose to indulge needs to be examined on a regular basis.

"You are ruled by your habits. It takes a habit to replace a habit. Develop positive habits that will work in harmony with the achievement of your definite purpose and goal." - Napoleon Hill

5. Think Long Term

Decision making becomes easier once you know where you are headed and you can make decisions

based on what will get your closer to that goal. Thinking long term will help you to choose an apple over a donut in the morning, working out instead of watching one more episode, and it'll help you avoid toxic people when choosing someone to date. It will help you decide if you should take that job or not. Keep your long term vision in mind in all your daily decision making.

6. Avoid Toxic People

10 toxic people to avoid: pessimists, the gossip, the temperamental, the victim, the self-absorbed, the envious, the manipulator, the judgmental, and the arrogant. Toxic people usually have behavior that are irrational, self-centered, and negative. These are easy traits to spot and distance yourself from. However, it's impossible to go through life and not deal with all of these people in way or another, at some point. The trick to handling a toxic person is to remain emotionally distant! Don't buy into their games. This is where personal awareness shows its power. Self-awareness is required to be emotionally distant enough to deal with these personalities.

"Once you've identified a toxic person, you'll begin to find their behavior more predictable and easier to understand. This will equip you to think rationally

about when and where you have to put up with them and when and where you don't. You can establish boundaries, but you'll have to do so consciously and proactively. If you let things happen naturally, you're bound to find yourself constantly embroiled in difficult conversations. If you set boundaries and decide when and where you'll engage a difficult person, you can control much of the chaos. The only trick is to stick to your guns and keep boundaries in place when the person tries to cross them, which they will." - Dr. Travis Bradberry

7. Pursue Your Passion

The big question I'm sure you're asking yourself is: what am I going to do with the rest of my life? For high-school seniors, this is usually matched with pressure from their parents and counselors: what major are you going to pick in college? Many times we hear stories of the pressure, from parents especially, to pick career paths that are lucrative but do not necessarily align with your passion or calling in life. From my own experience and talking to many other successful individuals, reaching success in ANY field or walk of life is difficult. You must be willing to pay the price: long nights, early mornings, sacrifice, stress, financial struggles, etc. There are always challenges on the road

to success, and sometimes, passion is the only fuel to get you to your destination. Following and investing in your passion is always the best route to follow. Design the life that you want, now. Follow your passion.

8. Make Someone Else's Life Better

Decide to make a difference in someone else's life. This has to be a decision that is made daily. To get you started on the habit, start small, and choose one person or kind act a day. Watch as your life is transformed from this practice. Your life will become better, by making others' lives better. We are all placed on this earth to make someone else's life better. Make this philosophy a way of life. Treat others how you would like to be treated. The world has a way of sending you the same energy that you put out. Live your best life by bringing out the best in those around you.

*"If you are not **making someone else's life better**, then you are wasting your time."* - **Will Smith**

9. Decide!

Just decide! Take the jump. Risk is an essential part of the progression. You can't steal second base with your foot on first. Once you've made your decision,

act! No looking back, no regrets. Once you've decided to move forward, more forward and never look back!

10. Never Give Up!

We are all on our own mission. We each have a unique purpose and path to destination purpose. Wherever that destination or purpose is, one thing is certain, you WILL be tested along the way. Have your made up your mind that you will move forward despite any obstacles that get thrown in your way or how hard the road gets. To survive and thrive on the road to purpose, mastery, and success, we must have strength in character. We must have the grit to get past the hard times. Having this mindset will equip you with the skills to persevere and find a passion for accomplishing your long term goals. Fail forward! Find the courage to keep pushing forward during failures and challenges. Follow through on the goals and vision you set for yourself. Remember to stay patient with yourself. Remain optimistic and be open to finding a creative solution or route to your success destination. Whatever you do: Never Give Up!

Closing Thoughts

"At some point, you make the scary decision to leave everything you're doing and go all in." – John Henry

The universe has a way of isolating us so that we can find ourselves. The universe isn't punishing you; it's isolating you so you can find your ultimate purpose. At first, it may seems like you've lost friendships and relationships but this is just part of the process of finding your purpose. But do not fear! For this is the ultimate treasure: finding your path, passion, and purpose! This is worth so much more than anything you will lose in the process. The beautiful thing about the transformation (said in hindsight, ask me this at 18-21- or 23 and I still wouldn't have this perspective), is that everything you lose will be gotten back times 10 over when you are living and breathing in your purpose. Your love life, friends, health, and wealth will all be replaced with the best and what's meant for you.

Popcorn and Success - 1:32

The path to success is a lot like making popcorn in the microwave. The first step is deciding that we want popcorn (success). Next, we must walk towards the area we know the popcorn to be. Unwrap a protective plastic layer, and then place the popcorn in

the microwave. Next, we must determine how much time we are willing to invest. If we don't invest enough time, we won't pop enough kernels to fulfill our potential, or worse, no kernels will reach their potential at all. If we invest too much time, we may burn the potential altogether. Once we select the right time, let's say 2-minutes for this example, we press start and the transformation process begins.

If we were to observe the transformation process, we will see the popcorn bag, highlighted in dim lighting...spinning around and around and around....dormant. 58 spins later and more than a minute has passed and there that popcorn bag is in the dim light spinning around and around....still dormant. I can only imagine how that popcorn bag must feel, she's been working so diligently and for an extended period of time, and she has nothing to show for it. If this popcorn bag was a quitter, she would be convinced she didn't have what it takes and stunt her potential.

Luckily, this bag is no quitter. So diligently, she keeps working. Around and around she goes. 30 more spins and still....dormant. Nothing to show for her efforts. Now she's hot! *"I'm working and working, I am doing everything right, where are the results*?" and if we are still observing this bag, we are also concerned. What

is going on? We placed the bag for 2 minutes and here we are at 1:30 and nothing. And Suddenly at 1:31...POP! We experience our first success! And slowly but surely, the success rolling in like the rivers of opportunity flow into the abundance of the success ocean.

POP!.........POP!.....POP! POP!...POP! POP! POP! POP!.

As we observe, the popcorn transformation is happening at an accelerated rate, and the bag itself is swelling up like a balloon. This step of expanding is necessary so it can hold all the new transformed kernels. And before we know it, DING! The 2 minutes is up, and the transformation process is done. Interestingly enough, as we go to grab the enlarged bag, wafting with a wonderfully buttery smell, we hear "Pop Pop....pop." Wow! Success is still happening, even after the process is over.

Success is a lot like making popcorn. When you start a new path, the first 75% will be the toughest. Only in the last 25%, when we're typically exhausted, will we experience the fruits of our labor. *"You've got what it takes, but it'll take everything you've got."*

The moral of the story: *Success if a process.* When you are working hard and not experiencing

success, just know you are somewhere between 1 second and 1:31. Your 1:32 is coming soon and before you know it, you'll have more transformation and abundance than you imagined. Understanding that we must expand in perspective and experience in order to grow in life, just like the bag had to expand to fit the new size of the popcorn. Soon, we will be filled with abundance and even experience some success when we're not trying anymore (the "Pop Pop...pop" after the Ding!).

Lastly, it's inevitable, every bag of popcorn has a few kernels that just failed to transform. This is okay, failure is just part of the process. You'll be so full of gratitude and success, you won't even notice the kernels that didn't manifest. Stay diligent, stick to your plan, and get to your 1:32.

"The purpose of life is to discover your gift. The meaning of life is to give it away. "- David Viscott

The End

Darnell Leatherwood

Dominating Life After High-School

Educator and Social Entrepreneur

Darnell Leatherwood is a doctoral candidate, Institute of Education Sciences (IES) fellow, and Illinois Board of Higher Education (DFI) fellow at the University of Chicago in the School of Social Service Administration. He holds a M.A. in the Social Sciences from the University of Chicago and a B.S. from the College of Business at the University of Illinois at Urbana-Champaign. In 2017, he started the Black Boys Shine campaign which is purposed to strengthen/control the Black male narrative and image nationally and internationally.

If you could go back in time, to your 18th birthday, what advice would you give yourself?
If I could go back in time, to my 18th birthday, the advice I would give myself is "do not hold back your excellence in public out of fear that you will intimidate others". For so long I did my course/school work alone, I worked out alone, I

dreamed alone, and all this to protect others from the weight of my personal expectations, capacity, and potential. Be excellent in public and build young one. Your excellence is not meant to drive away but to draw. Do not fear your power.

Advice for setting and accomplishing goals. In all things "do what you have to do so you can do what you want to do". For example, I pay my bills nine months in advance. I am proactive about accomplishing the "have to" (e.g., pay bills) so I can focus on the "want to" (e.g., financial freedom with remaining money). Additionally, I often tell my students that it is important that I create value right here in the moment. Yes, I set goals. Yes, I accomplish them. However, I do not get so wrapped up in the future that I forget to impact my today. Do excellence today, right now in the moment, and your tomorrow (your goals) will manifest just as they should. Also, I have a deep trust of the Most High. In all my intrinsic motivation, I have an

external locus of control based on my relationship with the Most High.

Advice on living a life of purpose and gratitude. When I give advice, I shy away from telling others what to do. As potentially evidenced in my aforementioned responses, I like to tell others what I would do and they take from that what they will. Everyone's situation is different, everyone has different preferences, and it would be foolhardy of me to tell you...in all your uniqueness what to do. That said, l live a life of purpose by following my heart and serving others. My heart tells me that my mission is to help others live better lives and I take this mission seriously. A note here, just in case you don't know what your purpose is, your purpose is probably the thing you most enjoy doing and that you do for free all the time. So to live on purpose one may find it valuable to chase one's passion. Finally, gratitude is a byproduct of understanding that one's purpose is not only meant for yourself but

has the real potential to impact others. I am forever grateful that I can be trusted to love on others in ways that may aid in them living the kind of life they dream of. My gratitude is in the service.

Dominating Life After High-School

Vanessa Abron

Founder/Director of Agency Abron

Vanessa Abron is a public relations professional with 14+ years of experience, and expertise in securing positive media coverage for brands in national and local media outlets. Vanessa's experience represents a broad range of public relations initiatives in a variety of industries, making her a valuable asset to any campaign. She accredits her success on her passion for continuously building positive relationships with a broad spectrum of individuals combined with her steadfast commitment to ensuring that the media, community and the client all receive mutually beneficial rewards from any project.

If you could go back in time, to your 18th birthday, what advice would you give yourself?

If I could go back to my 18th birthday, I would tell myself not to allow "adulting" to get in the way of my dreams. As we grow through the maturation period between being a teenager and an adult, we undergo a series of life setbacks that may challenge our beliefs in achieving the dreams we once had. I

would tell 18-year-old Vanessa not to let setbacks deter her from her path. I would remind her how awesome she is and tell her that she has what it takes to conquer the world. What has held me and many others back is a subconscious lack of confidence. Often it's not one big thing that shatters someone confidence, but it's several small moments that pick away it. Similar to how Andy Dufresne picked away at the escape hole he created in The Shawshank Redemption. Several little picks can make a massive hole over time. It could be criticism at a job, judgment from friends, failed expectations set upon you from family members, and so forth and so forth. So with all of that said, I would tell 18-year-old Vanessa not to allow those setbacks to keep her down.

Advice for time management.

For me, adequate rest is essential for my time management. Many believe that the formula is to work and work with little sleep. I believe the exact opposite. When you are well rested and focused, you can knock out more in four hours than you could in eight hours if you are exhausted during that

time. For me, an active to-list helps me stay on track and I establish daily, weekly and monthly goals.

How do you stay organized and on schedule with demanding schedules?

I make sure I put important dates on my calendar and I keep constant to-do lists. Once one is complete (or almost complete), I start a new one. I've also began meditating over the past year or so, and it's been amazing at helping me keep my mind fresh so I can stay on task and follow my intuition on what to move on next.

Ro'chelle Williams

Chief of Staff

Ro'chelle Williams is a seasoned political and education operative. Mr. Williams has worked for the Democratic National Committee, Brazile & Associates, LLC., the Climate Action Campaign and is currently at the National Education Association. He holds a Bachelors Degree in Political Science and a Master of Science in Higher Education Administration. He currently, resides in the nation's capital, Washington, D.C.

If you could go back in time, to your 18th birthday, what advice would you give yourself?

Make certain that you live life to the fullest and set goals for yourself. Those goals may be both short-term and long-term. Seek out those individuals that you wish you emulate. Surround yourself around like minded individuals, who help you grow and you help them grow. Stray away from becoming complacent. Always seek a deeper understand and never stop learning.

Dominating Life After High-School

Advice for time management.

Plan accordingly and make sure you have both a paper calendar and digital calendar (iPhone/Google calendar).

How do you stay organized and on schedule with demanding schedules?

Prioritize things by deadlines and importance. Make sure you have time during the day to review and respond to emails and phone calls. I have a planner and I have calendar planning meetings at work as well. It is equally important to be organized in life and in the work place. Without it, you will never be productive.

Dominating Life After High-School

Dania Corral

Management and Program Coordinator

Joined the Military as a senior in high school, and now works as a civilian federal employee for the US government. Entrepreneur and Photographer.

If you could go back in time, to your 18th birthday, what advice would you give yourself?

Take the risks and don't be afraid to walk away from things, places and people that are not aligned with your life. Don't let friends and family influence your decisions over your dreams and what you're capable of. It's ok to make mistakes just learn from them and don't hold onto them. Learn to let go of the things and people that hurt you. Stay positive, keep smiling and don't give up on your dreams. Travel the world and appreciate the little things in life like a long shower, a bed and a warm plate. Give to the less fortunate.

Advice for surviving & thriving in corporate America.

The things that make you different are the things that make you special and will also help people

remember you: Always do your best and be the hardest worker in the room.

Advice on social media etiquette? or How do you stand out on social media?

Don't post anything that can be used against you later.

Advice on etiquette in the workplace?

Always be professional and kind.

Monica Lopez

Human resources-organizational development professional, entrepreneur, speaker, influencer, and author.

Monica Lopez is a human resources-organizational development professional, entrepreneur, speaker, influencer, and author. Monica is passionate about empowering women to embrace their authenticity and build on their talent to design their professional experience that elevates them both personally and professionally. A true wonder woman and leader turning her many adversities into opportunities to expand her reach among women. She is an advocate for women fighting for equity in education and the workplace. Her experience in professional development and as a speaker has empowered women to take charge of their personal and professional development.

If you could go back in time, to your 18th birthday, what advice would you give yourself?

Do what you need to do now so you can do what you want later. i.e. Finish college as quickly as possible, save as much money, invest as much

money. Opportunity doesn't come knocking on your door, you have to know on it and sometimes kick that door open! When you have the moment where you feel like you don't know what you want to be when you grow up, remember you don't have to know it all right away, you just have to start with your passion. FYI We change what we want to be like 5x after we decided what we wanted to be in the first place! Why? Because were designed to grow and evolve.

Advice for surviving & thriving in corporate America.

Make time to build relationships, Look for opportunities to network, Join professional organizations internally at work and externally outside of work. Find opportunity in times of crisis i.e. when there is work to be done and no one wants to step up, be that person that steps up. Trust me you won't be forgotten, and its an opportunity to create something of your own without fear of judgement.

Advice on social media etiquette? or How do you stand out on social media?

Keep it professional, fun and make sure your content is valuable to your audience. Demonstrate your expertise by commenting on posts that align with your knowledge or skill set. Post during peak times such as morning, noon, and early afternoon. Choose a platform that works for you and gives you the most exposure.

Advice on etiquette in the workplace?

Always be last to speak, give feedback and respond according the energy in the room. Always be a team player and open to all ideas.

Anterio Jackson

Founder

Born in Chicago, Illinois. Proud graduate of the University of Illinois Urbana-Champaign 2010. Anterio has mentored and helped over 500 students get into college with over 30 million in scholarships aid. He is a Board Certified credit consultant, Business Credit Certified Consultant and Financial Advisory.

If you could go back in time, to your 18th birthday, what advice would you give yourself?

Learn more about yourself and invest in real estate. Find a solid mentor and build a team of like-minded individuals.

Any general advice for how to handle or look at finances as a young adult?

List out all of your fixed and variable expenses and find what is a need vs want. Begin, to seek alternative services that you can get the same quality at a lower price. Everything that you spend your money on that does not give you a return on

your investment you are robbing yourself of your future in terms of your lifestyle.

Tips for trimming expenses & saving as a young adult?

To trim expenses what you have to do is live below your means. Having the most expensive items is not always a good thing, but it can be necessary depending on the items. Example: the average phone bill is about $80 a month.

$80 per month x12months=$960 a year
$960 x 5ycars= $4800 spent in 5 years

Get 5 Years of Cell Phone Service at one price of $589
That is less than $10 a month for 60 months!

$4800-$589=$4211 in Savings
That equates to $842.20 Saved per year!
Link to service: bit.ly/mcsusacell

That is one of many ways I help clients reduce expenses.

Dominating Life After High-School

Can you help me understand credit & how to use it to my advantage?

Credit is the ability of a customer to obtain goods or services before payment, based on the trust that payment will be made in the future. When someone lends you money, and you pay them back with interest, they have "extended you credit."

Credit is the ability to borrow money and manage it responsibly. Buy now, pay tomorrow.

A FICO Score is a credit score developed by FICO, a company that specializes in what's known as "predictive analytics," which means they take information and analyze it to predict what's likely to happen. (Fico Score Ranges from 300-850) SO! if you get 300 points by default all you have to work with is 550.

VantageScore is a consumer credit-scoring model, created through a joint venture of the three major credit bureaus (Equifax, Experian, and TransUnion).

Here's how to get the perfect credit score:

Payment History

35% of 550=
192.5 Points
Solution: Make 100% of your payments on time!

Utilization
30% of 550=
165 Points
Solution: Pay your credit card balance in full each month

Length/Age of Credit History
15% of 550=
82.5 Points
Solution: Have an average of 15 years on all accounts

Types of Credit
10% of 550=
55 Points
Solution: Have
1 installment, 1 revolving and 1 open-ended account

New Credit/Inquiries

10% of 550=
55 Points
Solution: Have zero inquiries

Jeff Badu

Certified Public Accountant

Jeff Badu is a serial entrepreneur and a wealth multiplier. He's a Licensed Certified Public Accountant (CPA) and the founder of Badu Enterprises, LLC, which is a multinational conglomerate that owns several key companies. His marquee company is Badu Tax Services, LLC, which is a CPA firm that specializes in tax preparation, tax planning, and tax representation for individuals and businesses.

If you could go back in time, to your 18th birthday, what advice would you give yourself?

I would save and invest more money.

Any general advice for how to handle or look at finances as a young adult?

Dominating Life After High-School

You have to keep the future in mind. Start now and you will finish early. It's never too early to start investing.

Tips for trimming expenses & saving as a young adult?

You have to have a budget at all times and analyze each month which of those expenses are needs and wants. Try to get rid of the wants or find a way increase your income to pay for your wants.

Can you help me understand credit & how to use it to my advantage?

Credit is one of those things that can help you advance in life or destroy you. You have to use it wisely. You need to have a credit card, but use it wisely. Always keep track of your credit report/score each month.

Vaughn L. Roland

Political Consultant

Vaughn L. Roland is a political consultant specializing in stakeholder engagement, message development, legislative education and public policy. Vaughn served as district representative for Congresswoman Robin Kelly (IL-02), where he led her Chicago office in outreach, constituent services, and policy engagement. Vaughn has also worked in a number of federal and local political campaigns.

If you could go back in time, to your 18th birthday, what advice would you give yourself?

Trust the process.

Tips for making a good impression.

Be prepared and dress to impress.

How do I become a more effective communicator?

Be a sponge to knowledge, practice, and put yourself in uncomfortable environments.

Dominating Life After High-School

Advice on strategically growing your network and maintaining relationships

Never be afraid of exiting your comfort zone, its typically where you find some of the most unforgettable and valuable lessons and experiences.

Serita Love

Founder of Success Junkie

Serita Love is an Englewood native from Chicago, mom and author who educates, motivates and inspires by combining book and street smarts. From speaking and volunteering to donating to causes that promote upward social mobility, she is on a mission to get people hooked on ambition. She grew up seeing people hooked on negative habits. Her mission is simply to get people hooked on positive habits that changes lives.

If you could go back in time, to your 18th birthday, what advice would you give yourself?

Learn everything you can about finances.

General dating advice for young adults.

Be yourself and do not try to be who you think that person wants you to be. Eventually your lies will catch up with you. Be honest and respect and be sure to command respect as well. Everyone isn't good at dating. You will have some great experience and some poor experiences. Just be sure to learn from all of them.

Communicate. When dating, text messaging isn't the best communication method for truly getting to know someone. Ladies: Give him a call. Fellas: Give her a call. Hearing the voice of someone you actually like is pretty cool. This message is coming to you from a person who doesn't like to talk on the phone. However, I enjoy to speaking to the person I am dating.

Enjoy the process. This simply means that titles aren't always necessary. Focus on being friends and if things are meant to get more serious, then they will. Fellas: If you want to moving forward with a young lady, let her know. Ladies love when a Man tells her what she wants. You can thank me later for that tip.

Don't rush. It's a recipe for disaster. Get to know the person you are dating. Do cool things together and learn about one another. The best thing about dating is the experiences that comes with it. Creative Dates are the best! So, have fun.

Dating Etiquette Tips for Men?

Being a gentleman isn't lame or out of style. Your first impression is very important! If you want to

shoot your shot, be direct and let her know that you're interested in getting to know her better. Confidence is key. If a woman can sense your lack of confidence, it won't be very attractive to her. If the interest is mutual, then it's time for you to get to planning your next move.

First dates are interesting, but you can do this. See when she is available. Learn some basic things about what she may and may not like. Then, make arrangements for you to to get together. Make plans to be somewhere that is familiar territory. You need to be comfortable, right? Show her a great time at one of your favorite spots.

Please be sure to smell great and be properly groomed before you plan to meet. You want her to like you, not run away from you. One thing most women loves is a great fragrance; especially on a man who treats us well. Make a note of it. If you don't know what fragrances women like the most, then ask other women. You can't go wrong.

When going out, open her door if she is in your car. Open all doors that you two both enter. Walk her to

her front doorstep if you drop her off to her place of residence. Take her to places where you can afford to pay the bill for the both of you. Unless you agree to go Dutch, be prepared to pay for the initial dates. Ask open ended questions to get to know her. If you like her, let her know. Be the first to reach out via text or phone call. Take the lead. Ladies love a man with a vision.

If you feel like she doesn't really like you, ask her. It's ok to fall back if you do not feel like there is any real chemistry. It's better to know earlier on than later. Rejection is not that bad. Just be sure to follow you gut.

When you are spending quality time, limit the phone usage. If you need to be on your phone often, at least give her the courtesy of knowing why, so she doesn't think you are rude.

Here's an important tip for if she likes you and you know it: Keep pursuing her! Check in on her to let you know your'e thinking about her. Make plans for the next time you want to see her. Make her smile with small gestures. Do these things for her if she is receptive to it.

There are so many great things you can be mindful of while dating, but the tips will vary from woman to woman. Just get to know the woman you want to date. Over time, you will see whether sparks fly or if the chemistry is a dud.

Overall, bring your best self forward. Respect her and be considerate of the tings she tells you that she desires. Any woman who appreciates that about you might be a winner.

Best of luck!

Dating Etiquette Tips for Women?

Ladies, dating is fun and you have to make the best of it by doing a few things.

If you like this guy, give him the opportunity to take you out to get to know you. He may surprise you in unexpected ways. Be open to meeting somewhere that you will feel comfortable hanging out at. If you don't want him to pick you up from your place of residence, let him know. Meet him at the venue you agree upon and plan to have a great time.

I suggest you dress to impress. You don't have to wear anything revealing, but make sure your look

highlights you best features. Whatever look makes you feel the most confident is probably the best look to go for. Men love a confident women, so show up in a way that makes him smile from ear to ear.

If you like a good fragrance like me, add some when you go on dates. Men love when a women smells lovely. Wear "just enough" and not too much. You don't want your scent to be overwhelming. If you don't like fragrances, just be sure you smell fresh. Also, respect his time. Be on time to meet and if you are running late, tell him in advance.

Please do not talk about exes, babies, marriage on first dates. Talk about him. Show interest. Be positive and speak your mind, but do not dominate the conversation. And if you drink, not drink too much. Doing so, is tacky. Don't do that.

And another thing: Put your phone away. Nothing is worse than a man sitting with a women glued on her phone like she is bored. It's rude and distasteful. Have some respect form yourself and that man. If you absolutely need to be on your phone or have it near, just let him know. I'm sure he will understand.

Don't chase the guy. You are supposed to be pursued. Let him reach out to you more often than you reach out to him. Dating requires balance and you are the prize. If he really likes you, you will know by his actions.

When it comes to the bill, at least be willing to subtly offer to pay. You can reach for your purse or offer to pay the tip. Most men will not be offended at the gesture. But, be prepared to cover your portion when going out; especially for first dates. If he declines your offer, thank him for covering the expense and proceed with your evening.

The best dating etiquette tip I can provide any woman with, is this: Respect that man. Respect his time, his wallet and his energy that he places into getting and maintaining your attention. Do not play any games. Be direct. Show appreciation and if it's meant to be something more serious, it will be. Follow your heart and dating will be everything you want and more.

Dominating Life After High-School

Cassius L. Rudolph

Theologian, Scholar, Community Organizer

The Reverend Cassius L. Rudolph currently serves as the Executive Director of the People's Consortium for Human and Civil Rights Inc. Before this appointment he served as the National Field Director of the Rainbow/PUSH Coalition and Special Assistant to the Reverend Dr. Jesse L. Jackson, Sr. He is also a lecturer at Tougaloo College within the division of humanities. A national leader on the theological scholarship of Black Liberation Theology, Rudolph delivers sermons, lectures, and workshops throughout the United States

If you could go back in time, to your 18th birthday, what advice would you give yourself?

The advice I would give my 18 year old self would be to take risks and become the best at being you! As life has progress so far, I am happy with the outcomes and the roads I have traveled to get to where I am today.

Advice: How to handle transitioning from Highschool to College.

Dominating Life After High-School

The best advice to handle transitioning from HS to College is to make sure you visit the campus that you will reside on for the next 4 years to get a lay of the land, learn the ins and outs, and learn your peers.

Advice: How to handle transitioning from College to Adult Life.

Simple: Just do it! As you near the end of your college career, prepare for either graduate school or a career.

Kevin Itima

Commercial Real Estate Broker

Kevin Itima was born in Houston, Texas graduated from Jackson State University with a Bachelor's degree in Psychology, Magna Cum Laude and finished his Master in Public Administration from the University of Houston. His education, specifically his masters helps him understand how local government policy affect the housing stock and profitability for investors. His interest in real estate was sparked by his father who encouraged his curiosity and set the example by buying investment properties in Nigeria.

Kevin is an entrepreneurial real estate investment professional with extensive full lifecycle project management and oversight expertise within highly competitive markets. Kevin has a talent for identifying and sourcing revenue-generating investment opportunities and potential new business prospects. Throughout his career, he has been recognized for an ability to bridge the technical world of real estate with the customer-facing world of sales and marketing.

Dominating Life After High-School

If you could go back in time, to your 18th birthday, what advice would you give yourself?

Learn how to effectively network and market. Intentionally create networks that will make it easier to excel in your future careers. Don't be afraid to ask for help and say you don't understand something.

Advice for living on your own for the first time?

Keep your expenses as low as possible. Make sure you are honoring your financial obligations like paying rent on time and bills. Never put yourself in a situation in which you'll need someone else's help to bail you out.

Rent vs. Own, what should I do? (Benefits vs Negatives)

Owning a home can be a great financial, but owners need to understand it is not a status symbol but a way to create wealth. This means individuals should refrain from purchasing more than a house is worth, making unnecessary cosmetic upgrades, or purchasing something that they can't afford long term.

Renting allows an individual to be flexible with life decision and explore what they truly want in a permanent home. However, if you already plan on being in a city long term and are moving into your earlier 30's it is time to start considering and preparing to buy. You'll likely be saving money on a mortgage and creating a de facto retirement savings of sorts.

I'm 18 but I want to be a homeowner soon, advice?

Build credit, work history, savings, and understand what you want in a home you may be living in for 10-30 years.

Shala Akintunde

Artist and Producer

Shala is a Nigerian artist and pioneer in the medium of Solar Art; a practice that merges art and solar technology. He is lauded for his Seven Spoon portrait series and Shala's Bronzeville Solar Pyramid; a sculpture that generates photovoltaic electricity using his unique art-rendered solar

giclees -- making his Chicago landmark the first public sculpture of its kind.

If you could go back in time, to your 18th birthday, what advice would you give yourself?

Who you are matters. Give yourself permission to be great.

I like to live on my own terms, any advice on designing your life?

Life is not about finding yourself. Life is about creating yourself. The more responsibility (response-ability) you take for your life the more power you will have. Period.

How do I get over the fear or failure...and the fear of success?

Fail. Fail Fast. Fail hard. Fail often. Look for failures like they are successes and you will win often and big! Trust me. Why? Because it's the best way to learn and confront what does not work. It's counter-intuitive and that is why winners win so often. They know the cheat-code. Failing is the step before winning.

You cannot really win if you do not confront your real underline fears. As you fail, you will confront what really scares you --- looking bad, being confronted by your belief that you are not good enough or possibly the loss of love. You cannot deal with these things if you do not confront them through failure.

Real winners also know that people love success stories. Those stories are even better when people see you fail first. People love to relate. "Came from the bottom and now we are here!" In short, simply, fail! Fail Fast. Fail hard. Fail often.

I hear every successful person has struggles, do you mind sharing one of yours and how you've learned from it?

My main struggle was my belief that I was not good enough and ultimately believing that I did not matter beyond what I could provide for people. I did not believe that I could deserve love just for being who I am. I spent a good amount of my life working for outside validation. I was managing artists instead of being one. I always thought they were better than I was. I believed I was not good enough.

This did not allow me to see and enjoy my own unique talent.

Fortunately for me, I have always been into learning new things and bettering myself. I read a lot and started getting really curious about why I was always working so hard to be accepted by my peers. When I became aware of my limiting belief and the fact that I had made it all up in my head, I began to practice believing that I was the only one great at being me. Since I made up one belief I figured I could make up another one. This time I made up a story that works for me! Since no one else could be as good at being me as I could I no longer catered to the idea of not being good enough. It was irrelevant.

I had bad habits associated with my former belief so I took on new habits and told everyone I could to hold me accountable. I asked people not to let me see the insecure stuff I used to say and I surrounded myself with people that believed in me. I put myself around people that celebrated me instead of tolerated me. I began growing my art practice into the unique contribution it is now. I have been successful ever since.

THE IDEAL CANDIDATE
Dominating Life After High-School

Michelle Little

Program Manager, Early College & STEM Initiatives

Michelle Little is the Program Manager of Early College and STEM Initiatives at Sarah Goode STEM Academy. Mrs. Little made the transition to this role from the 9th grade English classroom where she successfully prepared freshman students to thrive throughout high school by teaching them the skills they would need to be successful. She received her Bachelor's degree in English from the University at Albany in upstate New York where she then went on to attain her Master's of Science in Secondary Education before moving to Chicago.

If you could go back in time, to your 18th birthday, what advice would you give yourself?

If I could go back in time to my 18th birthday I would tell myself to genuinely do things for myself without worrying what other people were doing, or what people would think. I would enjoy every minute of my teenage years and early twenties and be a bit more selfish (in a good way!).

THE IDEAL CANDIDATE
Dominating Life After High-School

Dress For Success Tips! (General or work related)

It sounds cliche but you really have to dress for the job or position you WANT, not necessarily the one you have. People's first impression of you usually has a lot to do with what you are wearing. You have the choice to either make this work for you or against you.

Why is dressing for success important and how has it impacted your life?

I've always taken pride in how I look and dress. Some people may call it shallow or live by the phrase "it's what's inside that counts" and although that is true, people won't pay attention to the inside or pay attention to you in general if they can't get past how you look or carry yourself on the outside. And dressing for success doesn't have to be expensive! Some of my clothes that I get complimented on the most are the least expensive items in my closet! I live by the saying...if you look good, you feel good, you do good, and it's all good!

Shelton Banks

Chief Executive Officer

Shelton Banks is a Chicago native from the Pullman/ Roseland neighborhood. He attended Morgan Park High School and was accepted into their International Baccalaureate program. After three years of schooling, he was forced into the workforce to care for his ill parent and household, yet, completed the GED program at Kennedy King College the same year. He entered the workforce as a part-time bank teller at National City Bank wherein less than three years he was promoted to a personal banker. Shelton went on to JP Morgan Chase, obtained his Series 6 and Series 63 investment licenses and became a VP Branch Manager in 2011.

After six years in the financial industry, Shelton pivoted his career into the technology sales industry at Groupon. After becoming a Business Development Manager, he went on to assist in launching Groupon's Mentorship Program and help to implement and take to market Groupon's new venture, BeautyNow. (Formally Pretty Quick) In 2017, Shelton was offered a position at Sprout

Social on their small business team. There he led and built a partnership with Goldman Sach's 10,000 Small Business Program with the goal of assisting small businesses in his community with their social marketing efforts.

Here is where Shelton met Harrison Horan, the founder of re:work training. After seeing the mission and vision of the organization, Shelton stated, "if this organization was around when I was growing up, I would have wanted to be a candidate." After volunteering with re:work training, Harrison could immediately see that Shelton was able to make a connection with candidates because of being in their shoes before. Shelton went on to interview and become the CEO of re:work training. Banks has now made it a goal to raise re:work's profile and bring on more national employers to help expand the programs reach.

If you could go back in time, to your 18th birthday, what advice would you give yourself?

I would tell myself that success does not always look the same. I didn't grow up with an abundance of role models. Often my family would preach to me as to what they thought I should be doing with

my life, which made it feel like everything outside their list was a completely not worth my time. That success "looks" like their ideas. I would tell myself that success changes on a daily bases and that it will not always look the same.

I like to live on my own terms, any advice on designing your life?

I look at job descriptions often of positions I do not think I am qualified for. I have learned that so many skills sets are transferable across dozens of industries. So as a look across essential functions and core competencies of different roles, I make it a point to add or learn piece in my current role, as a husband, father, friend and executive, so that me being qualified becomes a matter of time and not experience.

How do I get over the fear or failure...and the fear of success?

Fear, failure, and success all play a purpose. For me, failure is nothing but a learning experience. So is success. If you are the type of person that has worked had for everything you had, remember that at some point, you were at the bottom. The bottom

THE IDEAL CANDIDATE
Dominating Life After High-School

for me was a studio garden apartment eating Ramen noodles working a retail job. Was I a failure? I didn't and don't think so. Did I have a level of happiness? Yes. My thought process in moments of failure, is this worse than the basement? No, get over it. In moments of success I think, are you glad to be out the basement? Keep going.

I hear every successful person has struggles, do you mind sharing one of yours and how you've learned from it?

I didn't go to college. I dropped out of high school. I hate talking about it, especially around people that have went. High education has long dictated what success "looks" like. With every promotion, new job, and pay increase at times I feel like an imposter. Imposter syndrome! I grew up on the mantra "Fake it til you make it." I made it but at times I feel fake. I learned to own it. It's interesting how many people wish they could have done it like me, avoiding college debt. Those moments in telling my story help to continuously redefine what success can look like for me and others.

I wish I would have gave back sooner. For the longest time, I was fearful of helping people

because I feared the risk of someone else ruining my reputation. I especially felt like this being a minority in the tech space. A piece of what I was feeling is called stereotype threat, but another piece is rooted in what my family told me growing up, "NEVER CO-SIGN!" That person can hurt your credit. In the context of buy a car, sure, but in relation to a job or success...people have cosigned for me in the conversations that mattered, I should be willing to do the same.

"Success is the progressive realization of a worthy goal or ideal."

Earl Nightingale

How Happy Are You This Morning and Why?

1 2 3 4 5 6 7 8 9 10

_____

_____

_____

_____

I am grateful for…

1. _____

_____

2. _____

_____

3. _____

_____

My Ultimate Daily Goal

_____

_____

_____

_____

Top 3 Daily Tasks

1. _____

_____

2. _____

_____

3. _____

_____

How Happy Are You This Evening and Why?

1 2 3 4 5 6 7 8 9 10

_____

_____

_____

_____

Today I Learned...

_____

_____

_____

_____

3 Wins of the Day

1. _____

   _____

2. _____

   _____

3. _____

   _____

What Can I Improve?

_____

_____

_____

THE IDEAL CANDIDATE
Dominating Life After High-School

Visualize Your Future, What Do You See?

_____

_____

_____

_____

Disciplines Completed

Read 30 Minutes	(Check) _____
Exercise	(Check) _____
Personal Development	(Check) _____
Meditate/Visualize/Deep Breathing	(Check) _____

Tonight I Am Grateful For:

_____

_____

THE IDEAL CANDIDATE
Dominating Life After High-School

"Things work out best for those who make the best of how things work out."

John Wooden

How Happy Are You This Morning and Why?

1 2 3 4 5 6 7 8 9 10

_____

_____

_____

_____

I am grateful for...

1. _____

_____

2. _____

_____

3. _____

_____

My Ultimate Daily Goal

_____

_____

_____

_____

Top 3 Daily Tasks

1. _____

_____

2. _____

_____

3. _____

_____

How Happy Are You This Evening and Why?

1 2 3 4 5 6 7 8 9 10

_____

_____

_____

_____

Today I Learned...

_____

_____

THE IDEAL CANDIDATE
Dominating Life After High-School

_____

_____

3 Wins of the Day

1. _____

   _____

2. _____

   _____

3. _____

   _____

What Can I Improve?

_____

_____

The Ideal Candidate
Dominating Life After High-School

Visualize Your Future, What Do You See?

_____

_____

_____

_____

Disciplines Completed

Read 30 Minutes	(Check) _____
Exercise	(Check) _____
Personal Development	(Check) _____
Meditate/Visualize/Deep Breathing	(Check) _____

Tonight I Am Grateful For:

_____

_____

"Let no feeling of discouragement prey upon you, and in the end you are sure to succeed." Abraham Lincoln

How Happy Are You This Morning and Why?

1 2 3 4 5 6 7 8 9 10

_____

_____

_____

_____

I am grateful for...

1. _____

_____

2. _____

_____

3. _____

_____

My Ultimate Daily Goal

_____

_____

_____

_____

Top 3 Daily Tasks

1. _____

_____

2. _____

   _____

3. _____

   _____

How Happy Are You This Evening and Why?

1 2 3 4 5 6 7 8 9 10

_____

_____

_____

_____

Today I Learned...

_____

_____

_____

_____

3 Wins of the Day

1. _____

   _____

2. _____

   _____

3. _____

   _____

What Can I Improve?

_____

_____

Visualize Your Future, What Do You See?

THE IDEAL CANDIDATE
Dominating Life After High-School

_____

_____

_____

_____

Disciplines Completed

Read 30 Minutes	(Check) _____
Exercise	(Check) _____
Personal Development	(Check) _____
Meditate/Visualize/Deep Breathing	(Check) _____

Tonight I Am Grateful For:

_____

_____

"If you are not willing to risk the usual you will have to settle for the ordinary."

Jim Rohn

How Happy Are You This Morning and Why?

1 2 3 4 5 6 7 8 9 10

_____

_____

_____

_____

I am grateful for…

1. _____

_____

2. _____

_____

3. _____

_____

My Ultimate Daily Goal

_____

_____

_____

_____

Top 3 Daily Tasks

1. _____

_____

THE IDEAL CANDIDATE
Dominating Life After High-School

2. _____

_____

3. _____

_____

How Happy Are You This Evening and Why?

1 2 3 4 5 6 7 8 9 10

_____

_____

_____

_____

Today I Learned...

_____

_____

---

3 Wins of the Day

1. _____

   _____

2. _____

   _____

3. _____

   _____

What Can I Improve?

Visualize Your Future, What Do You See?

THE IDEAL CANDIDATE
Dominating Life After High-School

_____

_____

_____

_____

Disciplines Completed

Read 30 Minutes	(Check) _____
Exercise	(Check) _____
Personal Development	(Check) _____
Meditate/Visualize/Deep Breathing	(Check) _____

Tonight I Am Grateful For:

_____

_____

"When your life flashes before your eyes, make sure you've got plenty to watch."

Anonymous

How Happy Are You This Morning and Why?

1 2 3 4 5 6 7 8 9 10

_____

_____

_____

_____

I am grateful for...

1. _____

_____

2. _____

_____

3. _____

_____

My Ultimate Daily Goal

_____

_____

_____

_____

Top 3 Daily Tasks

1. _____

_____

2. _____

   _____

3. _____

   _____

How Happy Are You This Evening and Why?

1 2 3 4 5 6 7 8 9 10

_____

_____

_____

_____

Today I Learned...

_____

_____

---

3 Wins of the Day

1. _____

   _____

2. _____

   _____

3. _____

   _____

What Can I Improve?

Visualize Your Future, What Do You See?

THE IDEAL CANDIDATE
Dominating Life After High-School

_____

_____

_____

_____

Disciplines Completed

Read 30 Minutes	(Check) _____
Exercise	(Check) _____
Personal Development	(Check) _____
Meditate/Visualize/Deep Breathing	(Check) _____

Tonight I Am Grateful For:

_____

_____

Dominating Life After High-School

"The more you lose yourself in something bigger than yourself, the more energy you will have."

Norman Vincent Peale

How Happy Are You This Morning and Why?

1 2 3 4 5 6 7 8 9 10

_____

_____

_____

_____

I am grateful for...

1. _____

_____

2. _____

_____

3. _____

_____

My Ultimate Daily Goal

_____

_____

_____

_____

Top 3 Daily Tasks

1. _____

_____

2. _____

_____

3. _____

_____

How Happy Are You This Evening and Why?

1 2 3 4 5 6 7 8 9 10

_____

_____

_____

_____

Today I Learned...

_____

_____

_____

3 Wins of the Day

1. _____

   _____

2. _____

   _____

3. _____

   _____

What Can I Improve?

_____

Visualize Your Future, What Do You See?

THE IDEAL CANDIDATE
Dominating Life After High-School

_____

_____

_____

_____

Disciplines Completed

Read 30 Minutes	(Check) _____
Exercise	(Check) _____
Personal Development	(Check) _____
Meditate/Visualize/Deep Breathing	(Check) _____

Tonight I Am Grateful For:

_____

_____

"If your ship doesn't come in, swim out to meet it!"

Jonathan Winters

How Happy Are You This Morning and Why?

1 2 3 4 5 6 7 8 9 10

_____

_____

_____

_____

I am grateful for...

1. _____

_____

2. _____

_____

3. _____

_____

My Ultimate Daily Goal

_____

_____

_____

_____

Top 3 Daily Tasks

1. _____

_____

2. _____

_____

3. _____

_____

How Happy Are You This Evening and Why?

1 2 3 4 5 6 7 8 9 10

_____

_____

_____

_____

Today I Learned...

_____

_____

_____

_____

3 Wins of the Day

1. _____

   _____

2. _____

   _____

3. _____

   _____

What Can I Improve?

_____

_____

Visualize Your Future, What Do You See?

THE IDEAL CANDIDATE
Dominating Life After High-School

_____

_____

_____

_____

Disciplines Completed

Read 30 Minutes	(Check) _____
Exercise	(Check) _____
Personal Development	(Check) _____
Meditate/Visualize/Deep Breathing	(Check) _____

Tonight I Am Grateful For:

_____

_____

Dominating Life After High-School

"Courage is being scared to death, but saddling up anyway."

John Wayne

How Happy Are You This Morning and Why?

1 2 3 4 5 6 7 8 9 10

_____

_____

_____

_____

I am grateful for...

1. _____

_____

THE IDEAL CANDIDATE
Dominating Life After High-School

2. _____

_____

3. _____

_____

My Ultimate Daily Goal

_____

_____

_____

_____

Top 3 Daily Tasks

1. _____

_____

THE IDEAL CANDIDATE

Dominating Life After High-School

2. _____

_____

3. _____

_____

How Happy Are You This Evening and Why?

1 2 3 4 5 6 7 8 9 10

_____

_____

_____

_____

Today I Learned...

_____

_____

THE IDEAL CANDIDATE
Dominating Life After High-School

_____

_____

3 Wins of the Day

1. _____

   _____

2. _____

   _____

3. _____

   _____

What Can I Improve?

_____

_____

Visualize Your Future, What Do You See?

_____

_____

_____

_____

Disciplines Completed

Read 30 Minutes	(Check) _____
Exercise	(Check) _____
Personal Development	(Check) _____
Meditate/Visualize/Deep Breathing	(Check) _____

Tonight I Am Grateful For:

_____

_____

"Opportunity is missed by most people because it is dressed in overalls and looks like work."

Thomas Edison

How Happy Are You This Morning and Why?

1 2 3 4 5 6 7 8 9 10

_____

_____

_____

_____

I am grateful for...

1. _____

_____

2. _____

_____

3. _____

_____

My Ultimate Daily Goal

_____

_____

_____

_____

Top 3 Daily Tasks

1. _____

_____

2. _____

_____

3. _____

_____

How Happy Are You This Evening and Why?

1 2 3 4 5 6 7 8 9 10

_____

_____

_____

_____

Today I Learned...

_____

_____

THE IDEAL CANDIDATE

Dominating Life After High-School

____

____

3 Wins of the Day

1. ____

____

2. ____

____

3. ____

____

What Can I Improve?

____

____

Visualize Your Future, What Do You See?

THE IDEAL CANDIDATE
Dominating Life After High-School

_____

_____

_____

_____

Disciplines Completed

Read 30 Minutes	(Check) _____
Exercise	(Check) _____
Personal Development	(Check) _____
Meditate/Visualize/Deep Breathing	(Check) _____

Tonight I Am Grateful For:

_____

_____

"The only place where success comes before work is in the dictionary."

Vidal Sassoon

How Happy Are You This Morning and Why?

1 2 3 4 5 6 7 8 9 10

_____

_____

_____

_____

I am grateful for...

1. _____

_____

2. _____

_____

3. _____

_____

My Ultimate Daily Goal

_____

_____

_____

_____

Top 3 Daily Tasks

1. _____

_____

2. _____

_____

3. _____

_____

How Happy Are You This Evening and Why?

1 2 3 4 5 6 7 8 9 10

_____

_____

_____

_____

Today I Learned...

_____

_____

---

3 Wins of the Day

1. _____

_____

2. _____

_____

3. _____

_____

What Can I Improve?

_____

_____

Visualize Your Future, What Do You See?

_____

_____

_____

_____

Disciplines Completed

Read 30 Minutes	(Check) _____
Exercise	(Check) _____
Personal Development	(Check) _____
Meditate/Visualize/Deep Breathing	(Check) _____

Tonight I Am Grateful For:

_____

_____

THE IDEAL CANDIDATE
Dominating Life After High-School

"Capital isn't scarce; vision is."

Sam Walton

How Happy Are You This Morning and Why?

1 2 3 4 5 6 7 8 9 10

_____

_____

_____

_____

I am grateful for...

1. _____

   _____

2. _____

_____

3. _____

_____

My Ultimate Daily Goal

_____

_____

_____

_____

Top 3 Daily Tasks

1. _____

_____

THE IDEAL CANDIDATE
Dominating Life After High-School

2. _____

_____

3. _____

_____

How Happy Are You This Evening and Why?

1 2 3 4 5 6 7 8 9 10

_____

_____

_____

_____

Today I Learned...

_____

_____

---

3 Wins of the Day

1. _____

_____

2. _____

_____

3. _____

_____

What Can I Improve?

Visualize Your Future, What Do You See?

THE IDEAL CANDIDATE
Dominating Life After High-School

_____

_____

_____

_____

Disciplines Completed

Read 30 Minutes	(Check) _____
Exercise	(Check) _____
Personal Development	(Check) _____
Meditate/Visualize/Deep Breathing	(Check) _____

Tonight I Am Grateful For:

_____

_____

THE IDEAL CANDIDATE
Dominating Life After High-School

"Failure defeats losers, failure inspires winners."

Robert T. Kiyosaki

How Happy Are You This Morning and Why?

1 2 3 4 5 6 7 8 9 10

_____

_____

_____

_____

I am grateful for…

1. _____

_____

THE IDEAL CANDIDATE
Dominating Life After High-School

2. _____

_____

3. _____

_____

My Ultimate Daily Goal

_____

_____

_____

_____

Top 3 Daily Tasks

1. _____

_____

2. _____

_____

3. _____

_____

How Happy Are You This Evening and Why?

1 2 3 4 5 6 7 8 9 10

_____

_____

_____

_____

Today I Learned...

_____

_____

---

3 Wins of the Day

1. _____

   _____

2. _____

   _____

3. _____

   _____

What Can I Improve?

Dominating Life After High-School

Visualize Your Future, What Do You See?

_____

_____

_____

_____

Disciplines Completed

Read 30 Minutes	(Check) _____
Exercise	(Check) _____
Personal Development	(Check) _____
Meditate/Visualize/Deep Breathing	(Check) _____

Tonight I Am Grateful For:

_____

_____

"A goal is a dream with a deadline."

Napoleon Hill

How Happy Are You This Morning and Why?

1 2 3 4 5 6 7 8 9 10

_____

_____

_____

_____

I am grateful for...

1. _____

    _____

THE IDEAL CANDIDATE
Dominating Life After High-School

2. _____

   _____

3. _____

   _____

My Ultimate Daily Goal

_____

_____

_____

_____

Top 3 Daily Tasks

1. _____

   _____

THE IDEAL CANDIDATE
Dominating Life After High-School

2. _____

_____

3. _____

_____

How Happy Are You This Evening and Why?

1 2 3 4 5 6 7 8 9 10

_____

_____

_____

_____

Today I Learned…

_____

_____

_____

3 Wins of the Day

1. _____

   _____

2. _____

   _____

3. _____

   _____

What Can I Improve?

_____

_____

Visualize Your Future, What Do You See?

THE IDEAL CANDIDATE
Dominating Life After High-School

_____

_____

_____

_____

Disciplines Completed

Read 30 Minutes	(Check) _____
Exercise	(Check) _____
Personal Development	(Check) _____
Meditate/Visualize/Deep Breathing	(Check) _____

Tonight I Am Grateful For:

_____

_____

"Expect the best. Prepare for the worst. Capitalize on what comes."

Zig Ziglar

How Happy Are You This Morning and Why?

1 2 3 4 5 6 7 8 9 10

_____

_____

_____

_____

I am grateful for...

1. _____

_____

2. _____

_____

3. _____

_____

My Ultimate Daily Goal

_____

_____

_____

_____

Top 3 Daily Tasks

1. _____

_____

2. _____

_____

3. _____

_____

How Happy Are You This Evening and Why?

1 2 3 4 5 6 7 8 9 10

Today I Learned...

_____

_____

3 Wins of the Day

1. _____

_____

2. _____

_____

3. _____

_____

What Can I Improve?

_____

_____

Visualize Your Future, What Do You See?

_____

_____

_____

_____

Disciplines Completed

Read 30 Minutes	(Check) _____
Exercise	(Check) _____
Personal Development	(Check) _____
Meditate/Visualize/Deep Breathing	(Check) _____

Tonight I Am Grateful For:

_____

_____

THE IDEAL CANDIDATE
Dominating Life After High-School

*"Success is liking yourself, liking what you do,
and liking how you do it."*

Maya Angelou

How Happy Are You This Morning and Why?

1 2 3 4 5 6 7 8 9 10

_____

_____

_____

_____

I am grateful for...

1. _____

_____

2. _____

_____

3. _____

_____

My Ultimate Daily Goal

_____

_____

_____

_____

Top 3 Daily Tasks

1. _____

_____

2. _____

_____

3. _____

_____

How Happy Are You This Evening and Why?

1 2 3 4 5 6 7 8 9 10

_____

_____

_____

_____

Today I Learned…

_____

_____

THE IDEAL CANDIDATE
Dominating Life After High-School

_____

_____

3 Wins of the Day

1. _____

   _____

2. _____

   _____

3. _____

   _____

What Can I Improve?

_____

_____

Visualize Your Future, What Do You See?

THE IDEAL CANDIDATE
Dominating Life After High-School

_____

_____

_____

_____

Disciplines Completed

Read 30 Minutes	(Check) _____
Exercise	(Check) _____
Personal Development	(Check) _____
Meditate/Visualize/Deep Breathing	(Check) _____

Tonight I Am Grateful For:

_____

_____

THE IDEAL CANDIDATE
Dominating Life After High-School

"Success is walking from failure to failure with no loss of enthusiasm."

Winston Churchill

How Happy Are You This Morning and Why?

1 2 3 4 5 6 7 8 9 10

_____

_____

_____

_____

I am grateful for...

1. _____

_____

2. _____

_____

3. _____

_____

My Ultimate Daily Goal

_____

_____

_____

_____

Top 3 Daily Tasks

1. _____

_____

2. _____

_____

3. _____

_____

How Happy Are You This Evening and Why?

1 2 3 4 5 6 7 8 9 10

_____

_____

_____

_____

Today I Learned...

_____

_____

THE IDEAL CANDIDATE
Dominating Life After High-School

---

3 Wins of the Day

1. _____

_____

2. _____

_____

3. _____

_____

What Can I Improve?

Visualize Your Future, What Do You See?

_____

_____

_____

_____

Disciplines Completed

Read 30 Minutes	(Check) _____
Exercise	(Check) _____
Personal Development	(Check) _____
Meditate/Visualize/Deep Breathing	(Check) _____

THE IDEAL CANDIDATE
Dominating Life After High-School

Tonight I Am Grateful For:

_____

_____

"The function of leadership is to produce more leaders, not more followers."

Ralph Nader

How Happy Are You This Morning and Why?

1 2 3 4 5 6 7 8 9 10

_____

_____

_____

_____

THE IDEAL CANDIDATE
Dominating Life After High-School

I am grateful for...

1. _____

_____

2. _____

_____

3. _____

_____

My Ultimate Daily Goal

THE IDEAL CANDIDATE
Dominating Life After High-School

_____

_____

_____

_____

Top 3 Daily Tasks

1. _____

   _____

2. _____

   _____

3. _____

   _____

How Happy Are You This Evening and Why?

1 2 3 4 5 6 7 8 9 10

_____

_____

_____

_____

Today I Learned...

_____

_____

_____

_____

3 Wins of the Day

1. _____

_____

2. _____

_____

3. _____

_____

What Can I Improve?

_____

_____

Visualize Your Future, What Do You See?

_____

_____

_____

_____

Disciplines Completed

Read 30 Minutes	(Check) _____
Exercise	(Check) _____
Personal Development	(Check) _____
Meditate/Visualize/Deep Breathing	(Check) _____

Tonight I Am Grateful For:

_____

_____

"Big pay and little responsibility are circumstances seldom found together."

Napoleon Hill

How Happy Are You This Morning and Why?

1 2 3 4 5 6 7 8 9 10

THE IDEAL CANDIDATE
Dominating Life After High-School

_____

_____

_____

_____

I am grateful for…

1. _____

_____

2. _____

_____

3. _____

_____

THE IDEAL CANDIDATE
Dominating Life After High-School

My Ultimate Daily Goal

_____

_____

_____

_____

Top 3 Daily Tasks

1. _____

_____

2. _____

_____

3. _____

_____

How Happy Are You This Evening and Why?

1 2 3 4 5 6 7 8 9 10

_____

_____

_____

_____

Today I Learned…

_____

_____

_____

_____

3 Wins of the Day

1. _____

_____

2. _____

_____

3. _____

_____

What Can I Improve?

_____

_____

Visualize Your Future, What Do You See?

_____

_____

THE IDEAL CANDIDATE
Dominating Life After High-School

_____

_____

Disciplines Completed

Read 30 Minutes	(Check) _____
Exercise	(Check) _____
Personal Development	(Check) _____
Meditate/Visualize/Deep Breathing	(Check) _____

Tonight I Am Grateful For:

_____

_____

"People with goals succeed because they know where they're going."

THE IDEAL CANDIDATE
Dominating Life After High-School

Earl Nightingale

How Happy Are You This Morning and Why?

1 2 3 4 5 6 7 8 9 10

_____

_____

_____

_____

I am grateful for...

1. _____

_____

2. _____

_____

3. _____

_____

My Ultimate Daily Goal

_____

_____

_____

_____

Top 3 Daily Tasks

1. _____

_____

2. _____

_____

3. _____

_____

How Happy Are You This Evening and Why?

1 2 3 4 5 6 7 8 9 10

_____

_____

_____

_____

Today I Learned...

_____

_____

THE IDEAL CANDIDATE
Dominating Life After High-School

_____

_____

3 Wins of the Day

1. _____

_____

2. _____

_____

3. _____

_____

What Can I Improve?

_____

_____

Visualize Your Future, What Do You See?

_____

_____

_____

_____

Disciplines Completed

Read 30 Minutes	(Check) _____
Exercise	(Check) _____
Personal Development	(Check) _____
Meditate/Visualize/Deep Breathing	(Check) _____

THE IDEAL CANDIDATE
Dominating Life After High-School

Tonight I Am Grateful For:

_____

_____

"Identify your problems but give your power and energy to solutions."

Tony Robbins

How Happy Are You This Morning and Why?

1 2 3 4 5 6 7 8 9 10

_____

_____

_____

_____

THE IDEAL CANDIDATE
Dominating Life After High-School

I am grateful for…

1. _____

   _____

2. _____

   _____

3. _____

   _____

My Ultimate Daily Goal

_____

_____

THE IDEAL CANDIDATE
Dominating Life After High-School

Top 3 Daily Tasks

1. _____

   _____

2. _____

   _____

3. _____

   _____

How Happy Are You This Evening and Why?

1 2 3 4 5 6 7 8 9 10

_____

_____

Today I Learned...

_____

_____

_____

_____

3 Wins of the Day

1. _____

_____

2. _____

_____

3. _____

_____

What Can I Improve?

_____

_____

Visualize Your Future, What Do You See?

_____

_____

_____

_____

Disciplines Completed

Read 30 Minutes	(Check) _____
Exercise	(Check) _____

| Personal Development | (Check) _____ |
| Meditate/Visualize/Deep Breathing | (Check) _____ |

Tonight I Am Grateful For:

_____

_____

"Success usually comes to those who are too busy to be looking for it."

Henry David Thoreau

How Happy Are You This Morning and Why?

1 2 3 4 5 6 7 8 9 10

_____

_____

_____

_____

I am grateful for…

1. _____

   _____

2. _____

   _____

3. _____

   _____

My Ultimate Daily Goal

_____

_____

_____

_____

Top 3 Daily Tasks

1. _____

   _____

2. _____

   _____

3. _____

   _____

How Happy Are You This Evening and Why?

THE IDEAL CANDIDATE
Dominating Life After High-School

1 2 3 4 5 6 7 8 9 10

_____

_____

_____

_____

Today I Learned...

_____

_____

_____

_____

3 Wins of the Day

1. _____

_____

2. _____

_____

3. _____

_____

What Can I Improve?

_____

_____

Visualize Your Future, What Do You See?

_____

_____

_____

_____

THE IDEAL CANDIDATE
Dominating Life After High-School

Disciplines Completed

Read 30 Minutes	(Check) _____
Exercise	(Check) _____
Personal Development	(Check) _____
Meditate/Visualize/Deep Breathing	(Check) _____

Tonight I Am Grateful For:

_____

_____

"Opportunities don't happen. You create them."

Chris Grosser

How Happy Are You This Morning and Why?

1 2 3 4 5 6 7 8 9 10

_____

_____

_____

_____

I am grateful for…

1. _____

_____

2. _____

_____

3. _____

_____

My Ultimate Daily Goal

_____

_____

_____

_____

Top 3 Daily Tasks

1. _____

_____

2. _____

_____

3. _____

_____

How Happy Are You This Evening and Why?

1 2 3 4 5 6 7 8 9 10

_____

_____

_____

_____

Today I Learned…

_____

_____

_____

_____

3 Wins of the Day

1. _____

_____

2. _____

_____

3. _____

_____

What Can I Improve?

_____

_____

Visualize Your Future, What Do You See?

THE IDEAL CANDIDATE
Dominating Life After High-School

_____

_____

_____

_____

Disciplines Completed

Read 30 Minutes	(Check) _____
Exercise	(Check) _____
Personal Development	(Check) _____
Meditate/Visualize/Deep Breathing	(Check) _____

Tonight I Am Grateful For:

_____

_____

THE IDEAL CANDIDATE
Dominating Life After High-School

"Don't be afraid to give up the good to go for the great."

John D. Rockefeller

How Happy Are You This Morning and Why?

1 2 3 4 5 6 7 8 9 10

_____

_____

_____

_____

I am grateful for…

Dominating Life After High-School

1. _____

   _____

2. _____

   _____

3. _____

   _____

My Ultimate Daily Goal

_____

_____

_____

_____

THE IDEAL CANDIDATE
Dominating Life After High-School

Top 3 Daily Tasks

1. _____

_____

2. _____

_____

3. _____

_____

How Happy Are You This Evening and Why?

1 2 3 4 5 6 7 8 9 10

_____

_____

_____

_____

THE IDEAL CANDIDATE
Dominating Life After High-School

Today I Learned...

_____

_____

_____

_____

3 Wins of the Day

1. _____

_____

2. _____

_____

3. _____

_____

Dominating Life After High-School

What Can I Improve?

_____

_____

Visualize Your Future, What Do You See?

_____

_____

_____

_____

Disciplines Completed

Read 30 Minutes	(Check) _____
Exercise	(Check) _____
Personal Development	(Check) _____
Meditate/Visualize/Deep Breathing	(Check) _____

THE IDEAL CANDIDATE
Dominating Life After High-School

Tonight I Am Grateful For:

_____

_____

"I find that the harder I work, the more luck I seem to have."

Thomas Jefferson

How Happy Are You This Morning and Why?

1 2 3 4 5 6 7 8 9 10

_____

_____

_____

_____

I am grateful for…

THE IDEAL CANDIDATE
Dominating Life After High-School

1. _____

   _____

2. _____

   _____

3. _____

   _____

My Ultimate Daily Goal

_____

_____

_____

_____

Top 3 Daily Tasks

1. _____

_____

2. _____

_____

3. _____

_____

How Happy Are You This Evening and Why?

1 2 3 4 5 6 7 8 9 10

_____

_____

_____

_____

THE IDEAL CANDIDATE
Dominating Life After High-School

Today I Learned...

_____

_____

_____

_____

3 Wins of the Day

1. _____

_____

2. _____

_____

3. _____

_____

What Can I Improve?

_____

_____

Visualize Your Future, What Do You See?

_____

_____

_____

_____

Disciplines Completed

Read 30 Minutes	(Check) _____
Exercise	(Check) _____
Personal Development	(Check) _____
Meditate/Visualize/Deep	(Check) _____

Dominating Life After High-School

Breathing	

Tonight I Am Grateful For:

_____

_____

"Try not to become a man of success. Rather become a man of value."

Albert Einstein

How Happy Are You This Morning and Why?

1 2 3 4 5 6 7 8 9 10

_____

_____

THE IDEAL CANDIDATE

Dominating Life After High-School

I am grateful for…

1.

2.

3.

My Ultimate Daily Goal

Top 3 Daily Tasks

1. _____

   _____

2. _____

   _____

3. _____

   _____

How Happy Are You This Evening and Why?

THE IDEAL CANDIDATE
Dominating Life After High-School

1 2 3 4 5 6 7 8 9 10

_____

_____

_____

_____

Today I Learned...

_____

_____

_____

_____

3 Wins of the Day

1. _____

_____

2. _____

_____

3. _____

_____

What Can I Improve?

_____

_____

Visualize Your Future, What Do You See?

_____

_____

_____

_____

Disciplines Completed

Read 30 Minutes	(Check) _____
Exercise	(Check) _____
Personal Development	(Check) _____
Meditate/Visualize/Deep Breathing	(Check) _____

Tonight I Am Grateful For:

_____

_____

"Stop chasing the money and start chasing the passion."

Tony Hsieh

How Happy Are You This Morning and Why?

THE IDEAL CANDIDATE
Dominating Life After High-School

1 2 3 4 5 6 7 8 9 10

_____

_____

_____

_____

I am grateful for…

1. _____

_____

2. _____

_____

3. _____

_____

THE IDEAL CANDIDATE
Dominating Life After High-School

My Ultimate Daily Goal

_____

_____

_____

_____

Top 3 Daily Tasks

1. _____

   _____

2. _____

   _____

3. _____

_____

How Happy Are You This Evening and Why?

1 2 3 4 5 6 7 8 9 10

_____

_____

_____

_____

Today I Learned...

_____

_____

_____

_____

THE IDEAL CANDIDATE
Dominating Life After High-School

3 Wins of the Day

1. _____

   _____

2. _____

   _____

3. _____

   _____

What Can I Improve?

_____

_____

Visualize Your Future, What Do You See?

_____

_____

Disciplines Completed

Read 30 Minutes	(Check) _____
Exercise	(Check) _____
Personal Development	(Check) _____
Meditate/Visualize/Deep Breathing	(Check) _____

Tonight I Am Grateful For:

"We can let circumstances rule us, or we can take charge and rule our lives from within."

Earl Nightingale

How Happy Are You This Morning and Why?

1 2 3 4 5 6 7 8 9 10

_____

_____

_____

_____

I am grateful for...

1. _____

_____

2. _____

_____

3. _____

_____

My Ultimate Daily Goal

_____

_____

_____

_____

Top 3 Daily Tasks

1. _____

_____

2. _____

_____

3. _____

_____

How Happy Are You This Evening and Why?

1 2 3 4 5 6 7 8 9 10

_____

_____

_____

_____

Today I Learned...

_____

_____

THE IDEAL CANDIDATE
Dominating Life After High-School

---

3 Wins of the Day

1. _____

_____

2. _____

_____

3. _____

_____

What Can I Improve?

Visualize Your Future, What Do You See?

THE IDEAL CANDIDATE
Dominating Life After High-School

_____

_____

_____

_____

Disciplines Completed

Read 30 Minutes	(Check) _____
Exercise	(Check) _____
Personal Development	(Check) _____
Meditate/Visualize/Deep Breathing	(Check) _____

Tonight I Am Grateful For:

_____

_____

"The opposite of courage in our society is not cowardice...it is conformity."

Earl Nightingale

How Happy Are You This Morning and Why?

1 2 3 4 5 6 7 8 9 10

_____

_____

_____

_____

I am grateful for...

1. _____

_____

2. _____

_____

3. _____

_____

My Ultimate Daily Goal

_____

_____

_____

_____

Top 3 Daily Tasks

1. _____

_____

2. _____

_____

3. _____

_____

How Happy Are You This Evening and Why?

1 2 3 4 5 6 7 8 9 10

_____

_____

_____

_____

Today I Learned…

_____

_____

_____

_____

3 Wins of the Day

1. _____

_____

2. _____

_____

3. _____

_____

What Can I Improve?

_____

_____

THE IDEAL CANDIDATE
Dominating Life After High-School

Visualize Your Future, What Do You See?

_____

_____

_____

_____

Disciplines Completed

Read 30 Minutes	(Check) _____
Exercise	(Check) _____
Personal Development	(Check) _____
Meditate/Visualize/Deep Breathing	(Check) _____

Tonight I Am Grateful For:

_____

_____

THE IDEAL CANDIDATE
Dominating Life After High-School

"If you are not willing to risk the usual, you will have to settle for the ordinary."

- Jim Rohn

How Happy Are You This Morning and Why?

1 2 3 4 5 6 7 8 9 10

_____

_____

_____

_____

I am grateful for...

1. _____

_____

2. _____

_____

3. _____

_____

My Ultimate Daily Goal

_____

_____

_____

_____

Top 3 Daily Tasks

1. _____

_____

2. _____

_____

3. _____

_____

How Happy Are You This Evening and Why?

1 2 3 4 5 6 7 8 9 10

_____

_____

_____

_____

Today I Learned...

_____

_____

_____

_____

3 Wins of the Day

1. _____

   _____

2. _____

   _____

3. _____

   _____

What Can I Improve?

_____

_____

THE IDEAL CANDIDATE
Dominating Life After High-School

Visualize Your Future, What Do You See?

_____

_____

_____

_____

Disciplines Completed

Read 30 Minutes	(Check) _____
Exercise	(Check) _____
Personal Development	(Check) _____
Meditate/Visualize/Deep Breathing	(Check) _____

Tonight I Am Grateful For:

_____

_____

THE IDEAL CANDIDATE
Dominating Life After High-School

"The ones who are crazy enough to think they can change the world, are the ones that do."

Anonymous

How Happy Are You This Morning and Why?

1 2 3 4 5 6 7 8 9 10

_____

_____

_____

_____

I am grateful for...

1. _____

_____

2. _____

_____

3. _____

_____

My Ultimate Daily Goal

_____

_____

_____

_____

Top 3 Daily Tasks

1. _____

_____

2. _____

_____

3. _____

_____

How Happy Are You This Evening and Why?

1 2 3 4 5 6 7 8 9 10

_____

_____

_____

_____

Today I Learned...

_____

_____

_____

_____

3 Wins of the Day

1. _____

   _____

2. _____

   _____

3. _____

   _____

What Can I Improve?

_____

_____

THE IDEAL CANDIDATE
Dominating Life After High-School

Visualize Your Future, What Do You See?

_____

_____

_____

_____

Disciplines Completed

Read 30 Minutes	(Check) _____
Exercise	(Check) _____
Personal Development	(Check) _____
Meditate/Visualize/Deep Breathing	(Check) _____

Tonight I Am Grateful For:

_____

_____

"All progress takes place outside the comfort zone."

Michael John Bobak

How Happy Are You This Morning and Why?

1 2 3 4 5 6 7 8 9 10

_____

_____

_____

_____

I am grateful for…

1. _____

_____

2. _____

_____

3. _____

_____

My Ultimate Daily Goal

_____

_____

_____

_____

Top 3 Daily Tasks

1. _____

_____

THE IDEAL CANDIDATE
Dominating Life After High-School

2. _____

  _____

3. _____

  _____

How Happy Are You This Evening and Why?

1 2 3 4 5 6 7 8 9 10

_____

_____

_____

_____

Today I Learned...

_____

_____

_____

_____

3 Wins of the Day

1. _____

   _____

2. _____

   _____

3. _____

   _____

What Can I Improve?

_____

_____

Visualize Your Future, What Do You See?

_____

_____

_____

_____

Disciplines Completed

Read 30 Minutes	(Check) _____
Exercise	(Check) _____
Personal Development	(Check) _____
Meditate/Visualize/Deep Breathing	(Check) _____

Tonight I Am Grateful For:

_____

_____

51897611R00163

Made in the USA
Middletown, DE
06 July 2019